W9-AGZ-980

DREAMS

An Introductory Guide to Unlocking the Secrets of Your Dream Life

DAVID FONTANA

ELEMENT

Shaftesbury, Dorset • Boston, Massachusetts
Melbourne, Victoria

© Element Books Limited 1999
Text © David Fontana 1990, 1995, 1999

First published as *Dreamlife*
in 1990 by Element Books Limited

This revised edition first published in Great Britain
in 1999 by Element Books Limited
Shaftesbury, Dorset SP7 8BP

Published in the USA in 1999 by Element, Inc.
160 North Washington Street, Boston, MA 02114

Published in Australia in 1999 by
Element Books and distributed by
Penguin Australia Limited
487 Maroondah Highway,
Ringwood, Victoria 3134

Designed for Element Books Limited by
Design Revolution, Queens Park Villa,
30 West Drive, Brighton, East Sussex BN2 2GE

ELEMENT BOOKS LIMITED
Editorial Director: Sarah Sutton
Editorial Manager: Jane Pizzey
Commissioning Editor: Grace Cheetham
Production Director: Roger Lane

DESIGN REVOLUTION
Editorial Director: Ian Whitelaw
Art Director: Lindsey Johns
Editor: Julie Whitaker
Designer: John Fowler

Printed and bound in Great Britain by
Bemrose Security Printing, Derby

British Library Cataloguing in Publication
data available

Library of Congress Cataloging in Publication
data available

ISBN 1-86204-667-0

CONTENTS

With love and thanks to my brother Kenneth,
who also cares about dreams.

PICTURE CREDITS

Mary Evans Picture Library: p.41 (Max Halberstadt, Courtesy of WE Freud, Sigmund Freud Copyrights); p.44.

INTRODUCTION

It is hard to imagine a more evocative opening sentence to a story than that used by Daphne du Maurier in her novel *Rebecca*, 'Last night I dreamt I went to Manderley again'. The words speak directly to our imagination because in dreams we enter into the world of the imagination, an altered state of awareness in which we trade everyday reality for a strange world full of infinite possibilities. A world in which the past, the future, the present, lose their boundaries. Sometimes in this world we appear much as we are now, sometimes as we were years ago, sometimes as we may be in the years to come. Magical landscapes open up before us, arising and dissolving as if at the wish of an enchanter. Familiar people act in weird, unfamiliar ways. Unknown people appear and we greet them as if we have always known them. Bizarre adventures unwind before us, with ourselves sometimes as actors and sometimes as spectators. In dreams we fly, we make war, we make love, we exercise incredible powers.

LEFT DREAMS ARE A VOYAGE INTO THE UNKNOWN, BUT WITH EXPERIENCE WE CAN LEARN HOW TO INTERPRET OUR DREAMS.

DREAMS AND WAKING LIFE

Dreams captivate us because of their refusal to be bound by the laws of waking life, because of their trick of turning wishes into reality, of taking us into a story instead of leaving us to experience it from the outside. Dreams turn us into magicians. They intrigue, they inspire. We marvel at their creative power, at the vividness of their imagery, at the way they far outdistance the things our imagination can produce in waking life.

At times, they even seem to represent a parallel existence, another life influenced by, yet distinct from, our waking experiences. Dreams dissolve the boundaries of normality, they challenge the way in which we see and think about the world, they show us that life may indeed be other than what we think it to be.

In a sense, dreams can outweigh even the most moving experience art or books or theatre can give us, because even the greatest drama demands of us that we suspend our disbelief. In dreams there is no such demand, because in many dreams there is no disbelief. However fantastic the dream events are to our waking minds, our dreaming self accepts them without question. We walk into a room we know each day of our waking lives and find it strangely altered, yet the dreaming self bats not a dreaming eyelid. We pick up a cup and it changes into a gun, we meet a friend and his face becomes that of an enemy, we run and our legs refuse to carry us, then moments later we are moving faster than a galloping horse. We commit incredible acts of folly and incredible acts of bravery. Nothing is implausible, nothing is incongruous. The dream makes its own rules, and we accept these rules as if they are the rules of existence itself.

LEFT IN THE HOURS OF SLEEP WE ENTER ANOTHER LIFE, CAUGHT UP IN OUR NEW LIFE AS IF WE ARE THE CHARACTERS OF ANOTHER PERSON'S FANTASY.

In the language of waking life, dreams are used as synonyms for states of great success or happiness. 'It worked like a dream,' we say. 'I had to pinch myself to make sure I wasn't dreaming.' 'I never dreamt is could be so wonderful.' Even in my wildest dreams I never imagined... ' 'You're my dream lover.' 'It's always been my dream to... ' 'I used to dream about days like this.' And so on.

ABOVE OUR DREAMS TAKE US INTO A DIFFERENT WORLD, UNRESTRICTED BY THE BOUNDARIES OF OUR WAKING LIFE.

Dreams are our way of upgrading mundane reality. In referring to this mundane reality, Omar Khayyam (in Edward Fitzgerald's inspired translation of the work) speaks for most of us when he says:

'Ah love, could thou and I with Fate conspire
To grasp this sorry Scheme of Things entire,
Would not we shatter it to bits – and then
Remould it nearer to the Heart's Desire!'

Well in dreams we can remould it. Once we enter their mysterious world we can indeed grasp the sorry scheme of things that waking life sometimes represents, and remake it close to how we would have it be.

Should we, in spite of this, still doubt the power of dreams, it is as well to remind ourselves that dreams intrude into waking life more emphatically than waking life intrudes into dreams. We may view our dreams as flimsy, fragile things that fade in the moment of waking, yet in dreams waking life is even more flimsy and fragile. It is customary in waking life to remember our dreams, yet rare in dreams to recall the events of waking life. And although waking life provides the raw material of our dreams, dreams can also provide the raw material for waking life, sometimes in particularly spectacular and epoch-making ways (*see* Chapter 3).

And yet, and yet... For there is a qualification, and an important one, to be set against these positive aspects of dreaming. It is that dreams can disturb as well as excite, terrify as well as delight. For if dreams make their own rules, then there is no safety for us in them. A pursuer can pass through a wall as easily as we can. He or she can intrude into the securest of sanctuaries. In dreams there is no guarantee of privacy, no guarantee of good triumphing over evil, no guarantee of escape.

Our gun can turn back into a cup just when we have most need of it, or it can spit out bullets to which our pursuers are impervious. Our friends can turn against us. Our legs can refuse to carry us, our voice can refuse to speak, our body can refuse to move.

For the dream can take away from us as readily as it gives. It can trick us, deceive us, menace us, fill us with such fear or sadness that the memory shakes us for days and even years to come. No matter how far-fetched the dream, the emotions it arouses can haunt us for half a lifetime. Dreams can threaten our security, disturb our peace, unsettle our picture of ourselves and of others. They can alarm us to the point where we feel terrified to re-enter sleep, can come between us and our work and our relationships. They can also remind us of our mortality and of the mortality of those we love and of the things we cherish.

Our dreams may be lit with joy or shrouded in gloom, may be peopled with angels or peopled with demons, may entice or repel, may bring us hope or bring us despair. To add to the confusion, we may find ourselves powerless to predict which of these opposites it is going to be. Sometimes during a happy phase in our lives our dreams may be filled with foreboding and menace. At other times, when our waking life is depressed and negative, our dream life may seem bright with optimism and hope. Try as we might, we may find it hard to see a link between our waking and our sleeping lives, between who I think I am and who my dreams think I am. And in the end, perhaps, we may find it hard to decide which of them represents the real us.

DREAMS AND THE CREATIVE MIND

It is little wonder, therefore, that across the centuries dreams have taken such a hold upon the popular imagination. From the beginning of recorded history people have discussed their dreams, written about them, searched them for meaning. They have woven them into the fabric of many enduring myths and legends, built around them gripping tales for children, drawn from them the inspiration for great works in both art and science. They have used them as warnings of disaster, as ways of seeing into the future. The *Bible* and some of the other great spiritual books of humankind are full of them.

In the Old Testament, for example, Joseph became rich and very powerful by virtue of his understanding and interpretation of dreams, while in the New Testament Joseph was warned about dangers to the infant Christ in a dream. In the Old Testament, God told Aaron and Miriam that if there was a true prophet among the Israelites 'I will speak unto him in a dream'.

In Islam, it is accepted that God can speak to men and women 'in the form of sights or visions when the qualified recipient is asleep or in a state of trance' (Abdalati, *Islam in Focus*, 1978).

The Buddhists, the Hindus, the Ancient Egyptians and the Ancient Greeks all prized the messages received in dreams. Both the *Odyssey* and the *Aeneid* refer to the Greek belief in the gate of ivory and the gate of horn, with true dreams issuing through the former and false dreams through the latter. In Aboriginal myths, the world was created

11

in the Dreamtime, while in the shamanic culture that once flourished throughout much of Asia and still survives in certain Tibetan Buddhist and American Indian practices, dreams and trance were thought to allow the shaman to receive knowledge of the future and of distant events, and to leave his or her body and travel in the spirit realms. And, should we attempt to dismiss all this as evidence of the working of superstitious or primitive minds, it is well to remind ourselves of the number of scientists in more modern times who confess that the inspiration for their work came to them in dreams (*see* chapter 3).

ABOVE THE ABORIGINAL PEOPLE OF AUSTRALIA BELIEVE THAT THEIR ANCESTRAL SPIRITS WALKED THE EARTH IN THAT REMOTE PERIOD OF TIME KNOWN AS DREAMTIME. DURING THIS PERIOD, THE CREATION OF THE WORLD TOOK PLACE.

DREAMING,
THE BRAIN AND
THE BODY

CHAPTER ONE

Let's start by looking at modern scientific methods of studying dreams. These studies tell us a great deal about the incidence and frequency of dreams during the hours of sleep, and about what happens to the physical body when we dream. By pinpointing the moments during sleep when dreaming is most likely to occur, they also allow us to wake people when dreams are taking place, and thus listen to accurate descriptions of the things they are dreaming about. This is a major advance, since dreams are notoriously difficult for most people to remember upon normal waking.

At this scientific level, we have learnt more about dreaming during the last three decades or so than ever before in human history. Most of this learning has been done in what are known as sleep (or dream) laboratories, special rooms where subjects sleep wired up to devices that measure physiological responses such as brain waves, heart beat, blood pressure, muscular activity and eye movements throughout the night. At certain points during the night these responses change in ways in which I shall discuss shortly, and if the subjects are woken up at these points they almost invariably report dreams.

REMEMBERING YOUR DREAMS

The vast majority of us never have the opportunity of going to sleep in a dream laboratory, so we have to find other ways to help us remember and record our dreams. With practice and the right techniques, you should soon be able regularly to remember at least one, and probably more, dreams every morning.

To remember your dreams, practise the following:

1   Take your dreams seriously. The motivation to remember your dreams is a vital first step.

2   Whenever you think of it, tell yourself during the day that you will remember the dreams you have that night. Don't try and 'force' this message on yourself. Simply state it as a matter of fact.

3   As you lie in bed preparing for sleep, repeat the message over and over. If this keeps you awake, decide on a certain number of repetitions (say about 12), and then stop and compose yourself for sleep.

14

RIGHT REMEMBERING YOUR
DREAMS IS THE FIRST STEP IN
WORKING WITH THEM.

4 When you wake in the morning (or in the night), don't change your physical position in bed. Stay just as you are.

5 Concentrate on the thoughts running through your head and/or upon the emotions you may be feeling. Hold them at the centre of your awareness. Often they will trigger dream memories.

6 Keep a notebook or a tape recorder by the bed, and write down these memories before they fade (*see* also pp.24–25). Use the *present tense* when doing so. This helps recall (particularly of emotions and feelings), and makes the dream experience more relevant and immediate.

ABOVE RECORD YOUR DREAMS IMMEDIATELY UPON WAKING.

15

7 Return to the dream memories as often as possible during the day, so that you can 're-enter' the dream much as you would a waking memory.

8 Don't become discouraged or impatient. Keep trying. It may take days or weeks, but success will come.

ABOVE SET YOUR ALARM TO GO OFF DURING REM SLEEP.

If you want a short-cut to success, set your alarm clock to go off three hours or so after the time you usually fall asleep. This usually coincides with the second period of REM sleep, so you are likely to wake in the middle of a dream. If this doesn't work, experiment by moving the alarm forward or backwards 15 minutes or so each night until you find the right time.

WHAT HAPPENS WHEN WE SLEEP?

Increasing interest was focused upon sleep research by the discovery that during the night a sleeping person experiences four different stages, or levels, of sleep as measured by brain waves and general physiological activity.

Within the first hour of sleep we disengage increasingly from the outside world and descend through the four gradually deepening levels until we reach level four, and what is in many ways our deepest sleep of the night. At this level breathing becomes slow and rhythmic; blood pressure, heart rate and body temperature decrease; physical movement becomes minimal; the electrical activity of the brain changes from its waking state; and bodily metabolism slows down markedly.

Somewhere around one to one-and-a-half hours into sleep the pattern alters, however, and we move back upwards through the levels until we reach level one again. Many of the physiological changes associated with the deep sleep of level four are now reversed. The pulse becomes faster and often irregular, respiration and blood pressure increase, metabolism and brain waves return nearer to their waking state, the body often changes position, and in males penile erection usually takes place. At this point, we seem on the verge of waking, yet paradoxically there is a marked decrease in muscle tone and it is often harder to arouse us now than it is during deep level four sleep, hence the term *paradoxical sleep*, which is sometimes used to describe this re-entry into level one sleep.

During paradoxical sleep, the eyes begin to move rapidly up and down and from side to side behind the closed eyelids. These rapid eye movements give paradoxical sleep its more usual title of *rapid eye movement* or REM sleep (another term for it is emergent sleep; levels two to four are usually referred to as NREM, or non-rem sleep), and it is, in fact, the onset of our first major nightly episode of dreaming. On some 80 per cent of the occasions when aroused at this point, subjects report vivid dreams. Normally, this first stage of REM sleep lasts no more than 5–10 minutes, after which the subject sinks once more into deeper sleep (though usually without reaching beyond level two or level three sleep at any time during the remainder of the night).

Subsequently NREM and REM sleep alternate with each other in approximately one to two hour cycles throughout the night, with usually some four to seven repetitions of the cycle. Each of the deep sleep states is progressively shallower (we may only reach the depth of level four sleep during the first period of NREM sleep), while each of the REM states is progressively longer, culminating in the longest period (20–40 minutes) just before waking. The average adult spends around one and a half hours in REM sleep each night, though this may decrease to around one and a quarter hours in old age (when level four sleep also decreases and may even disappear altogether). Newborn babies pass a

BELOW BLURRED, SHADOWY DREAMS COMMONLY OCCUR DURING NREM SLEEP.

17

great deal of their lives in this state (some 60 per cent of their total sleeping time), while, interestingly, premature babies pass even more (up to 70 per cent).

During the early years of scientific sleep research (the 1950s and 1960s), it was thought that all our dreaming takes place during REM sleep. We now know that this is not the case. Some 50 per cent or so of subjects roused during NREM sleep also report dreams, but these are of a different kind from REM dreams. During REM sleep, dreams are vivid and active (the typical magic picture-show that we associate with dreaming), whereas in NREM sleep around 40 per cent of subjects report what seem more like shadowy, indistinct thoughts, set in a muffled fog-bound world in which dim shapes move in and out of awareness, than real dreams.

Why Do We Sleep?

Unfortunately, sleep research still hasn't solved the question why we dream or even why we sleep. Theories abound. Some believe we sleep to conserve our energy. Another suggestion is that, as the hunger mechanism is suppressed during sleep, we sleep in order to conserve food supplies. A more psychological explanation has it that, as our learning processes are largely inactivated during sleep, this gives the brain a chance to reorganize and store more efficiently the information gathered during the day.

These theories apart, sleep is certainly a pleasant and relaxing experience for the great majority of us, and a logical explanation would therefore be that we sleep to help the body recuperate physically. However, there is no hard physio-logical or chemical evidence from

LEFT A CHILD SECRETES MORE GROWTH HORMONE
WHILE IT IS SLEEPING THAN WHEN IT IS AWAKE.

research that this is the case. Physiologically and chemically then, apart from the fact that some children seem to secrete more growth hormone during sleep than during waking hours, any changes that are observed during sleep seem to have relatively little to do with actual physical renewal. In fact, deep meditation can in some subjects produce more relaxation and greater changes in bodily metabolism than can even the most profound sleep. However, research shows that irritability, anxiety and poor concentration all increase dramatically after the loss of only one or two nights' sleep, which certainly points to sleep as having an important psychological function for the vast majority of us.

Also of interest is the fact that the brain produces less of two chemicals called serotonin and noradrenaline during sleep (and perhaps particularly during REM sleep). These chemicals play a part in the transmission of nerve impulses in the brain, and their reduction means that the body is less able to transmit external signals to the brain. Even more importantly, serotonin and noradrenaline may be involved in the control of body temperature and in such higher-order functions as attention and learning. So sleep could be there in order to give the brain a rest from producing these chemicals, and thus to allow it to be more refreshed and alert when it resumes full activity upon waking. However, just as likely, the opposite could be the case, and the production of serotonin and noradrenaline could be decreased in order to allow us to sleep. Moreover, since serotonin is also thought to suppress hallucinations, it is intriguing to argue that the reduction at least in serotonin during sleep is a deliberate move by the body to enhance our capacity to experience the hallucinations of dreaming. This suggests an even more intriguing argument, namely that perhaps we sleep partly *in order to dream*. Sleep, in other words, may be the servant of the dream.

Is there any other evidence to support this argument? Some laboratory experiments do in fact show that if we are deprived of sleep, we spend an increased amount of time in REM sleep on subsequent nights, as if it's more important to catch up on REM than on NREM.

It's hardly surprising therefore that the ancient peoples of the world supported the view that sleep was there for the purposes of dreaming. And dreaming, they concluded, was there for the purposes of allowing us to enter another world. In most occult and early spiritual traditions, something (the consciousness, the soul, the astral body – terms for it vary) leaves the body during sleep and is free to travel in this other world, fragmentary memories of which it brings back in the form of dreams.

SCIENTIFIC EXPLANATIONS OF DREAMING

Not surprisingly, many 'orthodox' scientists remain uninterested in research into out-of-body experiences, and into such, to them, fanciful notions as a part of the consciousness leaving the body. For them, even human consciousness is of relatively minor importance. Since there is no good scientific way in which consciousness can be explained, they prefer to regard it as a kind of biological accident. A by-product of more important biological functioning. If such orthodox scientists have no final answer to the riddle of consciousness or to the question of why we sleep, it is not surprising they have no final answer either to the question of why we dream.

The theories scientists put forward can be grouped under three main headings. We can call them respectively the neuro-physiological model, the learning/remembering model and the forgetting model.

THE NEURO-PHYSIOLOGICAL MODEL

This suggests that during REM sleep the brain stem spontaneously generates signals that stimulate sensory channels in the brain much as input from the senses stimulates them in waking life. The brain elaborates these signals into visual and auditory images, a kind of sensory mimicry that tricks the sleeper into believing he or she is having real experiences – in other words that tricks the sleeping person into experiencing dreams. Since in sleep we are deprived of regularizing information from outside our heads against which we can test our dream events, we accept these events as 'real', no matter how outrageous they may be. And outrageous they certainly are, since the signals generated in sleep by the brain stem are random and confused, unlike the ordered events presented to us by the waking world. The physiological model also suggests that, since the production of serotonin and noradrenaline is reduced during sleep, the brain processes information in a more confused way, and we thus lose in dreams our sense of self-awareness and critical judgement.

This model, however, makes the mistake (all too common in orthodox science) of confusing process with cause. That is, it may

21

ABOVE OUR DREAM IMAGES MAY ARISE FROM RANDOM AND SPONTANEOUS SIGNALS.

describe accurately enough the process that goes on in the brain during dreaming, but it does nothing to explain what causes this process in the first place, and why it is there at all – in other words, what sets it off and the reason for its existence. This confusion is rather like saying that since the engine is the mechanical device that powers the automobile, it must therefore also be the driver.

The model further fails to tell us why dreams contain such a strong narrative content. For all their bizarre nature, dreams are not a succession of incoherent, disconnected events, as we would expect if they were explicable solely in terms of the spontaneous firing of neurological signals in the brain stem. On the contrary, dreams tell stories. The events that dreams contain show development, one from another, and often carry a clear thread of apparent meaning. Dream events hang together, and do so in a way hard to account for simply in terms of spontaneous neurological activity.

THE LEARNING/REMEMBERING MODEL

This is really an extension of the neuro-physiological model in that it advances a reason why the brain stem fires off signals in REM sleep. According to this model, these signals activate higher areas of the brain and in doing so maintain and reinforce learnt material that has been stored in our memory during waking life, rather as going over and over this daily material maintains and reinforces it. They may also give the neurons and electrical circuits in the brain an opportunity to practise even during the hours of sleep. The dreams that we experience are the subjective experience of this reinforcement and maintenance activity.

However, this model is purely speculative – there is no hard evidence to back it up. Moreover, dreams seem to go way beyond a repeated and wearisome rehearsal of the events of waking life. Also, when they do relate to these events, they often transform, elaborate and distort them in a way that is likely to confuse rather than to reinforce and maintain waking memory.

THE FORGETTING MODEL

This model argues that REM sleep serves to remove unwanted data from the memory. So many things happen to us during the day that if we remembered them all our brains would soon become over-crowded, far too full to allow us to find anything we want or to allow us space to store any new bits of information that we really do need to remember.

Rather like a computer dumping unwanted programmes, therefore, the mind in sleep reduces the strength between brain neurons, thus allowing information to be lost. The sleeping mind experiences this dumping process in the form of dreams, but in fact, it is not really intended for our attention at all.

The forgetting model therefore gives us a reason why dreams are so hard to remember – we are not intended to remember them in the first place. Further, it suggests that it is probably harmful to make any attempt to remember them, because such an attempt is like hanging onto our household rubbish instead of allowing the refuse-men to take it away.

In support of this suggestion it is sometimes argued that work with people interned in concentration camps during World War II shows that some individuals who rarely remember dreams of any kind (even when woken during REM sleep) have adjusted better to the memory of their terrible experiences than have those who frequently report dreams, many of which still relate back to these experiences.

This is of course very much a chicken and egg argument. Is it because people who dump their dreams dump their unwanted experiences, or is it because people who have dumped their unwanted experiences no longer need to dream about them? A further objection to this argument is that in any case it is dangerous to generalize from certain very special cases to the population at large. There is no evidence to suggest that in general people who remember their dreams are less psychologically healthy than people who do not. Many psychologists in fact maintain that the weight of evidence points emphatically in the opposite direction.

KEEPING A DREAM DIARY

You will need to keep a dream diary if you want to work on your dreams. Keep paper and pencil by the side of your bed and record your dreams upon waking. Remember to put a date against each entry. Include as much detail as possible. As you gain practice and train yourself in dream recall, you will find more and more details come back to you.

ABOVE A DREAM DIARY IS LIKE A DAILY DIARY EXCEPT THAT IT RECORDS YOUR SLEEPING RATHER THAN YOUR WAKING ADVENTURES.

Write them down. They may be important when it comes to the later business of analyzing your dreams.

The following points will help you to keep your dream diary:

• Write down the dream events in their proper order. Although the events may appear unrelated to each other, once you begin the process of analysis, relationships often become very clear.

• Keep a careful note of the dream characters. Who was in your dream, and what did he or she do? If they remind you of someone you know in waking life, write this down. Don't trust to memory.

• If well-known scenery appears, record any differences between it and the same scenery in waking life. Were the doors/windows in the right place? Were the colours accurate? Was the size right? (This is particularly important if you want to develop lucid dreaming, see chapter 6).

24

- Similarly, record any differences between well-known people in the dream and in real life.

- Record any non-human characters that appeared in the dream (animals, angels or any inanimate objects) that behaved as if alive.

- Make a special note of any recurring events, themes or characters. Do they always occur/behave in exactly the same way?

- Note down all the colours you see.

- Note down your emotional responses to everything.

- Finally, don't trust to memory. When you read back over your dream diary you may find you have no recollection at all of having some of the dreams. However clear they seem at the time, write them down.

THE MYSTERY OF DREAMING STILL REMAINS

So orthodox scientific research, while telling us a great deal about what goes on physiologically and chemically in the brain and in the body generally during sleep and dreaming, leaves us with the overriding conclusion that both these states are still very mysterious indeed. Perhaps no traveller ever set off more blithely or with less preparation into the unknown than most of us set off each night into sleep. It was Shakespeare's *Hamlet* who spoke apprehensively of the dreams that might come to haunt us in the sleep of death, and that it was indeed the fear of these dreams that makes us cling to life. He might almost as readily have spoken of the dreams that come to haunt us in the sleep between sunset and sunrise. Alternatively, he might have spoken of both sets of dreams with anticipation and excitement. One thing is clear. We probably aren't all that much closer to providing the final answer to their mystery than were men and women in Shakespeare's own time.

SOME CONCEPTIONS AND MISCONCEPTIONS ABOUT DREAMING

However, the findings of orthodox science about dreaming do help us dismiss or support a number of the popular ideas that surround this mysterious state.

SOME PEOPLE NEVER DREAM?

It is true to say that some people never remember their dreams, but highly unlikely that there are people who do not dream at all. All the evidence suggests that we all dream every night, and that our dreaming follows a relatively set pattern. Even people who claim they have never dreamt in their lives report dreams when they are woken up in sleep laboratories at the appropriate times.

MOST DREAMS UTILIZE THE RIGHT SIDE OF OUR BRAINS?

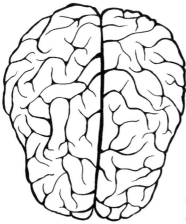

The brain is divided into two hemispheres, connected by a bundle of nerve fibres at the centre. We know that the left side, which controls the right side of the body, is concerned mainly with verbal, rational and analytical thinking, while the right side, which controls

LEFT DREAMS THAT ORIGINATE IN THE RIGHT HEMISPHERE ARE GENERALLY MORE IMAGINATIVE THAN THOSE OF THE LEFT SIDE.

the left side of the body, is more concerned with intuition, imagery and synthetic thinking. A common belief is that dreaming comes from the right side of the brain, hence its non-rational (and perhaps mystical) nature. However, studies with patients with right hemisphere impairment show they still dream. The left hemisphere does therefore have access to dreaming, though the dreams concerned tend to be unimaginative, utilitarian, more tied to reality and less symbolic than usual.

SOME PEOPLE DREAM ONLY IN BLACK AND WHITE?

If this is true, it is hard to explain. Colour is a dominant factor in our lives, and there is no obvious reason why the dreaming mind should choose to ignore it. Some surveys show that far more people claim to dream in black and white than in colour, but the truth is probably that such people forget the colour in their dreams more quickly than they forget other details. In sleep laboratories, people aroused during dreaming almost always report some memory of colour, however hazy. However, black and white dreaming does occur, if only rarely.

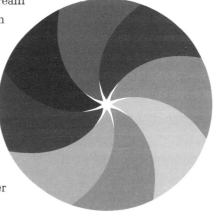

ABOVE MANY PEOPLE CLAIM TO DREAM IN BLACK AND WHITE, BUT IT IS LIKELY THAT WE DO DREAM IN COLOUR.

EVENTS IN DREAMS MAY SEEM TO TAKE A LONG TIME, BUT THE ACTUAL DREAM IS OVER VERY QUICKLY?

We pack a great deal of activity into dreams, mainly because they cut out those long pauses that take place between events in waking life. The dream does not waste time. It concentrates upon peak incidents, and the scenes it contains can change swiftly and dramatically. So in this sense time seems to be speeded up in dreams as compared to normal experience. But in real terms, dream adventures take as long to work themselves through as it would take you to imagine them in your waking life, and research shows that the episodes of dreaming can, in fact, be quite lengthy – anything up to 40 minutes or more in some cases.

ANIMALS DON'T DREAM?

We cannot be sure one way or another, but all the mammals so far monitored during sleep go through those physiological changes associated in humans with dreaming. They may also move their paws as if running, and growl and whimper as if experiencing dream adventures. So the evidence suggests they are dreaming.

BABIES DON'T DREAM?

Again we cannot be sure. But babies do in fact spend a very large part of their sleeping hours in REM sleep. As they grow older, the ratio of REM sleep to NREM sleep actually decreases. So babies would seem to be dreaming, though what on earth they are dreaming about is quite another matter.

DREAMS NEVER COME TRUE?

Dreams certainly reflect our waking hopes and fears for the future, and even keeping a cursory record of our dream life shows that sometimes these things come about and sometimes they do not. Much may depend upon the ratio between fantasy and reality that we put into our lives. But there may be more to it than

28

RIGHT BABIES ALMOST CERTAINLY DO DREAM THOUGH THE CONTENT OF THEIR DREAMS REMAINS A MYSTERY.

this. Can dreams in some way pick up knowledge about future events, even about future events of which we have no current information and therefore no current expectations?

WE DREAM LESS AS WE GROW OLDER?

Although the ratio of REM sleep to NREM sleep is particularly high in babies and declines a little later, this does not mean it goes on declining. We maintain a fairly stable pattern of REM to NREM sleep throughout most of our lives. The slight further decline when old age is reached may simply be because sleep patterns themselves tend to change in the elderly, with more naps being taken during the day and fewer hours of sleep at night. If the memory declines in old age, there may also be less tendency to remember dreams. But older people who stick to the sleeping habits of their younger days may stick to the same dreaming habits. It is impossible to generalize.

WE ARE MORE LIKELY TO REMEMBER THOSE DREAMS WE HAVE JUST BEFORE WAKING?

True. As we have seen, the longest session of REM sleep takes place in the period before waking. It is dreams from this final phase that are most likely to be recalled, though if we wake soon after going to sleep we may remember the dreams from an earlier phase.

YOU CANNOT CONTROL YOUR DREAMS?

People sometimes report dreaming about whatever happens to be on their mind as they are drifting off to sleep. So it's easy to assume you can decide the topic of your dream simply by holding it in your thoughts as sleep overtakes you. In practice, things are not as easy as that. You may in fact dream according to plan, but the dream is more likely to happen during your first cycle of dreaming, and not be remembered. Or, in the maddeningly perverse way that dreams have, your dreaming mind may choose to ignore the target altogether in favour of some apparently trivial event that happened earlier in the day. (This is in fact often found to be the case when subjects try to will their dreams during dream research, and are woken during the first dreaming cycle.) As we will see later, it is likely that you can gain a degree of control over certain aspects of your dreaming, but the task isn't an easy or a very precise one.

TALKING OR WALKING IN YOUR SLEEP INDICATES BAD DREAMS?

In actual fact, on being aroused sleep talkers and walkers rarely report they were dreaming, and both talking and walking take place mainly during NREM sleep. Their cause seems to lie in the sporadic firing of speech and motor mechanisms in the brain. The reason this happens in some people and not in others is unknown, but seems to be unrelated to the state of either one's dreaming or of one's conscience.

A BIG MEAL JUST BEFORE YOU GO TO BED BRINGS ON NIGHTMARES?

A heavy meal of any kind makes the digestion work overtime just when the whole body should be lowering its metabolism in order to relax and recuperate. The result, not surprisingly, is a restless night during which we wake several times, and are therefore much more aware of our early phases of dreaming than usual. The following morning we see these dreams as 'caused' by the heavy meal. However, if our full stomach actually leads to stomachache, this may prompt our dreams to be less pleasant than usual. There is evidence that the body's physical sensations

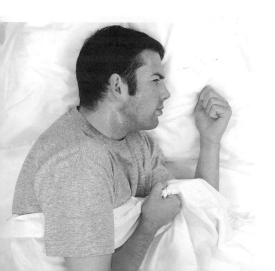

LEFT A RESTLESS NIGHT MAY RESULT IF THE BODY HAS TO WORK HARD TO DIGEST A LATE MEAL

during the night can influence dream content. A tight sheet, for example, may lead to dreams of being tied down, or the breeze from an open window may lead to dreams of being on the seashore or the prairies. The moral is a simple one – when we go to bed, our stomachs want to relax just like the rest of us.

SLEEPING ON YOUR BACK CAUSES NIGHTMARES?

People certainly snore more often when on their backs than when on their sides, but snoring is unconnected with dreaming. People sleeping on their backs are also more likely to feel the pressure of a full bladder. But in any case even the most restful of sleepers changes position a minimum of eight times during the night, so we are none of us likely to stay on our backs very long. Another myth that I first encountered in childhood is that you should never sleep on your left side as it makes your heart swell up and could kill you. In more recent years, I was intrigued to find that a particular Buddhist order instructs its monks always to sleep on their right sides, and since Buddhists know a thing or two I wondered if the myth could have some truth in it after all, however tenuous. That is until I shortly afterwards came across another order that instructs its monks to settle to sleep on their left sides. I'm not sure which order claims to keep their hearts in the best shape or to have the sweetest dreams.

31

BELOW PEOPLE WHO SLEEP ON THEIR BACKS ARE NO MORE PRONE TO NIGHTMARES THAN ANYONE ELSE.

MORE PEOPLE HAVE UNPLEASANT DREAMS THAN PLEASANT ONES?

In dream surveys more people do in fact report dreams involving aggressive acts and negative emotions such as anger, fear and sadness than friendly acts and positive emotions such as happiness, calmness and excitement. This may be because people are more inclined to remember negative dreams, or are more anxious to talk about them and discover their meaning. But since the dreaming mind seems to be concerned for much of the time with our waking problems, maybe this is just what we would expect. Dream research has shown, in addition, that depressed people tend to have more depressing dreams and anxious people more anxious dreams than do the rest of the population.

YOU DO NOT DREAM WHEN DRUNK?

Most drugs reduce the incidence of dreaming, and alcohol is no exception. To date, no drug that reliably enhances dreaming has been discovered. Some drugs appear to enrich the hypnagogic state (the state between waking and sleeping, *see* chapter 4) in that under their influence the images seen at this time take on a particular vividness and clarity, but whether this is because the drugs prolong this state, and thus give us more chance to be aware of it, or because they actually change its quality we do not as yet know.

FREQUENT SEX DREAMS REVEAL A HIGH SEX DRIVE?

It is true we tend to dream more frequently about the things that pre-occupy us. And some studies show that

LEFT DRINKING TOO MUCH ALCOHOL BEFORE GOING TO BED CAN SUPRESS OUR ABILITY TO DREAM.

sexual offenders have more dreams about violent sex than do the rest of us. So the frequency of our sexual dreams may tell us something about our sex drive. On the other hand they may simply tell us that our sex drive is being frustrated in some way (whether for good reasons or for bad). In adolescence, sex dreams – often with orgasm – are common in both sexes. Maybe frustration again plays some part, since sexual energy is high in adolescence while opportunity may be restricted. In adult life, erotic dreams are frequent during the early stages of sexual abstinence (as, for example, in those who enter monasteries), but tend to tail off after two years or so, as if nature gets the message that that particular bodily function is no longer required by its owner.

YOU CAN USE DREAMS TO SOLVE PROBLEMS?

Dreams themselves are highly creative experiences, and since problem-solving often demands a creative approach, it is logical that if we can bring at least some aspects of our dreaming under conscious control, we may be able to use it to help us with our waking problems. The evidence that we can indeed do so is strong (*see* chapter 3). (On a related subject, the evidence that we can learn during sleep by playing a tape to ourselves isn't strong at all, more's the pity.)

33

BELOW IF WE ARE FORTUNATE, OUR DREAMS MAY ACT AS AN OUTLET FOR OUR CREATIVE FUNCTIONING.

YOU DON'T CARRY YOUR MORAL CODE
INTO YOUR DREAMS?

In Freudian theory our moral sense, together with the rest of our conscious mind, nods off during sleep, leaving the unconscious mind, with all its amoral instinctive urges, to take over. The area awaits more research, but my own dreams show I'm perfectly capable of taking moral decisions consistent with my waking conscience while I'm asleep, and I've no reason to believe I'm unique in this.

CONCLUSION

The extent of these conceptions and misconceptions about dreaming (and the above list isn't exhaustive) is further evidence of the extent to which dreams intrigue us. They are part of our lives and yet not part of our lives. They represent the world and ourselves in a way so different from our waking experiences that it seems almost as if we live in two separate worlds, the world of waking life and the world of dreams. In the end, of course, remember that you are the best authority on this latter world. You are the person who nightly enters it. Many of the questions you ask about it are best answered by you yourself. You are your own dream explorer, your own dream researcher. Never believe it otherwise.

DREAM INTERPRETATION: ANCIENT AND MODERN

CHAPTER TWO

In ancient times, men and women took their understanding of life from direct experience. Dream events followed a different set of rules from waking life, therefore dreams were experiences of another kind of existence. No 'proof' was needed for this beyond the dream itself. Dreams were what they seemed to be. And since information was conveyed in dreams that appeared to be outside the waking experience of the dreamer, it followed that wise beings – gods perhaps – spoke to you in dreams. If the information conveyed was unpleasant, it followed that malign influences could also make use of dreams. The enigmatic content of dreams was recognized – whoever it was that spoke to you in dreams spoke in riddles, and left you to interpret their meaning for yourself. At the beginning of the 20th century, Sigmund Freud in one of the classic works on dreaming, *The Interpretation of Dreams*, identified two basic methods used by the ancients in dream interpretation. The first method took the dream as a whole and looked for an actual event that it might represent. The second method took each dream image as a separate sign, and looked for its individual, often symbolic meaning.

THE EARLY EGYPTIANS

As early as 2,000 BC the Egyptians were using both methods of interpreting dreams, and produced (in the so-called Chester Beatty papyrus) guidelines for applying them, many of which still influence the Dream Dictionaries on sale today.

For example, it was suggested that the whole dream could be interpreted in terms of opposites or contraries. An unhappy dream could therefore presage happiness, while a happy one could indicate the opposite. Individual images could be interpreted through association. If you dreamt, for example, of a shoe, and this suggested to your waking mind a boat and a journey over water, then just such a journey was either advisable or in fact lay ahead. Another possibility for individual interpretation was to use word similarities. If the word for the object of which you had dreamt sounded like the word for another object, then the dream was really about this second object, no matter how remote it seemed from the first. (An example from modern English would be to interpret a dream about a mouse as conveying a message about your house.)

Not content simply with interpreting dreams, the Egyptians also developed ways for trying to induce them. In the best known of these, the would-be dreamer took a special potion of herbs and slept in the temple.

36

LEFT THE ANCIENT EGYPTIANS USED HERBAL POTIONS TO INDUCE THE DREAMING STATE.

The following morning he or she recounted the night's dream to the priest, who then interpreted its meaning. Under the influence of the Egyptians, the Babylonians and the Jews developed similar systems, but the Jews also took account of the personality, the background, the economic circumstances and so on of the dreamer.

THE ANCIENT GREEKS

The ancient Greeks borrowed extensively from both the Egyptian and the Babylonian systems, but not surprisingly saw dreams as coming from their own rather than from Egyptian or Babylonian gods. They also copied the Egyptian method for inducing dreams, and a number of shrines were established, many of them associated with healing. The most important of these were the ones dedicated to Aesculapius of Epidaurus. It was common practice for a person to take a potion to induce sleep. The following morning his dream would be scrutinized by the priest as a guide to diagnosis and healing. If the dreamer was particularly fortunate, he or she might even be cured by the dream itself, particularly if the god Aesculapius actually appeared in the course of it.

By the fifth century BC, however, the Greek physician Hippocrates began to change the way in which the Greeks thought about dreams. Hippocrates argued that although they could be used in the diagnosis and treatment of disease, this was because they reflected bodily states rather than because they were messages from the gods. This thinking was further advanced in the third century BC when the philosopher Aristotle argued that if dreams really were messages from the gods, they would only be sent to wise people who could make proper use of them. His conclusion was that dreams were essentially sparked off by the senses. Thus, if one became too hot while asleep, one would have a dream about fire and so on. Due to the link between the senses and dreams, he agreed with Hippocrates that they could also serve as early indications of physical illness of one sort or another.

The Unconscious

The unconscious (sometimes wrongly called the subconscious) mind figures prominently in any discussion of dreams. In sleep, the conscious mind goes off duty, and the unconscious takes over and plays out our dreams for us. But what exactly is the unconscious? Psychologists talk of:

- The conscious mind – the things that are going through your head now.
- The pre-conscious mind – the information stored in your head that you can recall at will.
- The unconscious mind – forgotten and repressed material, instinctive drives: all those things stored away somewhere inside us that influence our behaviour but that we cannot access at will and that often (apart from in dreams) can only be brought up into our consciousness with the aid of special techniques.

One technique for getting in touch with your unconscious is hypnosis. Another is meditation (see pp.114–115). But a simple technique for you to try now is free association. In free association you can start with any word (an emotional or symbolic one is best) and allow it to set off a chain of associations in your mind that can lead to the sudden recall of long-forgotten memories or the upsurge of repressed emotion.

For example, start with the word 'water'. Hold it in your mind. What word or idea or image do you associate with it? Hold that in your mind and see what comes up next. Now what comes up in association with that word or image? Go on from there, allowing each association to spark off the next, no matter how far these associations lead you away from the original word. Try the same exercise using other words as your starting point. Do not be alarmed or frightened by what comes up. If negative, uncomfortable

> or even violent images surface, this does not mean that you are predominantly 'bad'. Everyone will experience these from time to time. They simply show that we have emotions or instincts or painful memories that we have never brought to the surface and laid to rest.
>
> Now back to dreaming. By accessing your unconscious in this way in your waking life, you will also bring yourself more in contact with your dream world. Sometimes dream memories surface in the course of free association. Dreams themselves become clearer, easier to remember and more meaningful.

The next important development occurred in the second century AD when the Roman Sophist Artemidorus proposed that dreams are in fact often a continuation of waking activities. Agreeing with the Jewish idea that dream interpretation must take into account the life circumstances of the dreamer, he produced no fewer than five books setting out guidelines for this interpretation. These books influenced most systems of dream interpretation right up until the time of Freud.

THE CHRISTIAN CHURCH

Although the trend away from the divine interpretation of dreams was partially reversed in the first centuries of Christianity (St John Chrysostum, St Augustine and St Jerome in the fourth century AD, for example, all taught that God reveals Himself in dreams), by medieval times the Church was firmly against the divine view. God's revelation was in and through the Church itself, and humans had no need of dreams or of any other kind of direct access to Him. Thomas Aquinas' advice was to ignore dreams as much as possible, while Martin Luther's was that at most they simply showed us our sins.

However, dreams were too strongly rooted in the popular imagination to be dismissed that easily, and with the growing availability of printed books from the 15th century onwards popular dream dictionaries (most based on the work of Artemidorus) began to proliferate. For all their naivete, these dream dictionaries fullfiled a useful function in that they took dream interpretation away from the priests and the seers who had traditionally controlled it, and suggested for the first time that each man or woman could be their own interpreter.

DREAMS AND THE UNCONSCIOUS

Although the importance of dreams was rejected outright by the scientific rationalism of the 18th century, which looked upon dream interpretation as just another form of superstition, few writers and poets were prepared to share this view, and dreams began to figure prominently in 18th- and 19th-century literature. Philosophers such as Fichte and Herbart began to take dreams seriously, and to see them as providing clues to the unconscious mind, theories about which were beginning to emerge from a number of quarters.

It was this link between dreams and the unconscious that was primarily responsible for the beginning of what we might call the scientific investigation of dreams. That is, an investigation that tried systematically to link dreams to underlying psychological and physiological causes, and to discover their significance, if any, for our psychological lives.

Gone was any attempt to link dreams to the word of God, or to use them for divining the future or in the diagnosis and treatment of physical illness. In their place was the growing conviction that dreams, along with all other psychological phenomena, are caused in some way by physical processes, and that careful observation would eventually reveal the exact nature of this cause. It was against this background that in late 1899 Freud's monumental work, *The Interpretation of Dreams*, made its appearance.

FREUD AND THE
INTERPRETATION OF DREAMS

Though he summarized the work on dreams that had been carried out over the centuries, Freud believed that virtually alone and unaided he had actually solved, once and for all, the mystery surrounding dreaming. 'Insight such as this,' he wrote in the preface to the third English edition of his book, *The Interpretation of Dreams*, 'falls to one's lot but once in a lifetime.' Indeed his book must be listed as one of the very few books that has changed the Western way of looking at the human mind.

ABOVE FREUD'S CONTRIBUTION TO DREAM ANALYSIS IS MONUMENTAL.

The Interpretation of Dreams did two things. Firstly, it established in the minds of many people that dreams deserve scientific study and analysis. Secondly, as is true of Freud's work as a whole, it made clear

41

FREUD AND DREAMWORK

The work of Sigmund Freud proposed that we ask the following questions of dreams:
- What is the cause and the purpose of dreams?
- How should we interpret their meaning?
- How should we use this interpretation to understand more about the psychological life of the dreamer?
- How can this understanding help us in diagnosing and treating psychological problems?
- How can further dreams be used to monitor the progress of this treatment?

the kind of questions we should ask during this study and analysis, though without necessarily providing the right answers.

Like Hippocrates, Freud believed that dreams do give clues to our state of health, although in his case it was primarily *psychological* health that was involved, and not physical health.

Freud came to the conclusion that dreams are essentially *wish fulfilment*. In his theory of human psychology, Freud considered we are each born with strong instinctive drives that operate initially at an unconscious level, and that govern our emotional responses and provide us with our fundamental motivation in life. Chief amongst these drives, and from which even our nobler forms of behaviour arise through sublimation, are the ones for personal survival (the *self-preservation drive*) and for the survival of the species (the *sex drive*). The former manifests itself in such things as self-assertion and anger and aggression, and the latter in sexual arousal and intercourse. Although not 'bad' in themselves, problems arise in human psychology when the emotional energy associated with these instincts becomes excessively frustrated or punished.

This happens particularly in childhood, where children are taught to conform to the rules and regulations of the adult world, with the result that the child has to control and repress many of the things that their instincts strongly motivate them to do. Self-assertion, for example, is typically discouraged in the child, as is any expression of sexuality. The result is that the emotional energy behind these drives, instead of being acknowledged and consciously channelled into socially acceptable forms, becomes repressed and disowned.

However, repressed energy does not simply go away. It persists at an unconscious level, from where it seeks an outlet when the controlling conscious mind is off its guard. Thus, in sleep, when the conscious mind relinquishes its control, the repressed energy seeks expression and gratification in the form of dreams; in other words it fulfils those wishes that have not been allowed expression at a conscious level. Our repressed resentment or hostility towards others, for example, and our repressed sexual desires, act themselves out in the theatre of sleep, allowing the repressed energy a necessary form of release.

But although it relinquishes control, the conscious mind still remains alert enough to wake up in the face of what it perceives as a threat of some kind, whether from the outside world or from disturbing experiences in our own dreams. Should the dream act out its fantasies in too blatant a manner, the conscious mind sees this as a threat to its moral sense, and accordingly wakes up (as can often happen, for example, in nightmares or in sexual dreams). Therefore in order to allow us to stay asleep and continue dreaming, the unconscious expresses these fantasies in a largely disguised, symbolic form – hence the strange and often apparently meaningless character of our dreams.

In Freud's view, this symbolic form shows remarkable consistency across cultures and between individuals, so much so that he considered it forms a universal symbolic language. A language that occurs not only in dreams but in such other deep outpourings of the unconscious as the great myths and legends of humankind. A language, moreover, that the psychotherapist can learn and, rather like the Egyptian priest, use in his or her interpretation of the client's dreams and the psychological states that underlie them.

43

For Freud, dreams thus have both a manifest content (what they seem to be) and a latent content (what they really are). If we are to use dreams to help understand the unconscious processes that in Freudian theory are seen to underlie most psychological disorders, we must therefore unravel the latent content of the dream, the hidden meaning that lies behind the manifest content. Dreams are, Freud argued, 'the royal road to the unconscious'. By unravelling their latent meaning we are able to bring to the surface the unconscious material that is causing our psychological disorders, and start the process of owning it and coming to proper terms with it.

To help in this unravelling, Freud developed the technique we used on pp.90–92, namely free association. Through his clinical experience, he discovered that the technique was particularly effective with patients if he took as the starting point the images or ideas that occurred spontaneously in their dreams. This procedure became one of the cornerstones of psychoanalysis and is still one of the most widely used methods for working with neurotic problems.

Freud's theory of dreams reflected his belief in the vital role played in the development of our personalities by the self-preservation and the sexual instincts respectively. Which brings me to a vital caution in any approach to dream understanding and dream analysis. Namely that it is all too easy to read into dreams one's own particular theoretical persuasion as to the nature of mind and of human personality. Due to their extraordinary variety and richness, one can all too readily see in dreams what one wants to see, and Freud, like many other dream interpreters, was not immune to this weakness. To offer one single explanation of dreams and of dream interpretation is as unrealistic as to offer a single explanation for the varied richness of waking experience. But Freud performed an invaluable service in drawing attention to the psychological importance of dreaming, and from Freud onwards no psychodynamic psychologist (that is, no psychologist concerned with unconscious processes and with the view that human psychology is driven by deep emotional forces) has neglected dreaming.

44

THE WORK OF CARL JUNG

Of all such psychologists, Carl Jung is perhaps the outstanding example. Jung's theories on dreams differed from those of Freud in that he saw the unconscious as the seat, not only of the self-preservation and sexual drives identified by Freud, but

LEFT CARL JUNG INTRODUCED THE CONCEPT OF THE COLLECTIVE UNCONSCIOUS, OF WHICH ARCHETYPES ARE THE CONTENTS.

also of higher motivational drives such as creativity and spirituality. Thus, dreams are not simply wish fulfilments of our repressed desires, but also the language in which our higher, wiser self can speak to us. In dreams we find the key not only to what is causing our present problems, but also to what we most need to do to put them right and to develop our full potential as human beings. Dreams are thus primarily a compensatory mechanism – they compensate for the errors and omissions in our conscious understanding.

Jung described each of us as living in a splendid house, yet seldom moving out of the basement. That is, we are full of potentialities – for creative expression, for experience, for achievement, for spiritual and psychological growth – which we not only fail to explore but of whose very existence we often live and die in complete ignorance. In dreams we find a means of discovering some of the other rooms in our house. In dreams we leave the basement and wander the vast corridors and staircases of our mind, sometimes discovering secret, unpleasant dark rooms that fill us with fear and anxiety, sometimes finding rooms full of useless lumber, but sometimes opening doors to rooms filled with sunlight and beauty, whose windows look out onto sweeping magical landscapes criss-crossed with roads and pathways leading towards the sunrise and the distant hills.

Just as we find many rooms in our house, so we meet many people. Some of them familiar, some of them strange and unknown. Some of them friendly, some of them apparently menacing and hostile. All of them have something to teach us. As we begin to read and understand our dream symbols so we become able to listen to this teaching. For Jung, as for Freud, the dream is deeply symbolic, containing both a manifest and a latent meaning. Dreams should not be taken at their face value. Few things in dreams are what they seem. If they were, we would risk being overwhelmed by what they have to tell us. Dreams reveal their secret messages to us in proportion to the ability of our conscious mind to understand and cope with them. Dream interpretation is a slow process, fraught with error and misunderstanding, but this in a sense is for our own protection. If we were confronted too abruptly with our hidden self, the conscious mind could well be swept away by it.

Like Freud, Jung encouraged his clients to provide free associations to the ideas and images in dreams in order to unlock their symbolic meaning. But unlike Freud, Jung did not encourage his clients to wander too far during free association from the dream itself. His advice was always to keep coming back to the dream symbol. Losing sight of the symbol, Jung believed, risked losing sight of the dream's real meaning, and becoming lost in free associations that in the end might have little to do with this meaning. The symbol itself held the key, and the mind must not be allowed to sidetrack into involved free associations and thus avoid confronting the deep issues that the symbol represented.

Jung also took a deep interest in the great myths and legends of humankind, and in the symbols used in the world's religions (such as the cross, the circle, the star, the eagle, the lion). Through an understanding of these outpourings of the creative human imagination, we can learn the language of dreams. Each man and woman is free to invent his or her own symbols (usually at an unconscious level), but the symbols we each of us invent usually show a remarkable similarity. For Jung, this was because we inherit not only our physical and mental characteristics, but also a *collective unconscious*, that is, an innate tendency to organize and interpret our experience in similar ways to each other.

The content of the collective unconscious is expressed primarily in symbols, or, as Jung called them, *archetypes*. Archetypes are thus primeval images and ideas, meaningful for all peoples and at all times, and found not only in myths and legends but also in children's fairy stories and in artistic

LEFT CERTAIN SYMBOLS, SUCH AS THE CROSS, ARE COMMON TO MANY DIFFERENT CULTURES AND BELIEFS.

46

expression. We each of us can modify and personify these archetypes in our own way, but easily recognizable examples include the wise old man, the witch, the trickster (who constantly challenges us and upsets our plans and our complacency), the hero, the beautiful woman, the magician and the wise animal. Many of our dream symbols are only understandable in terms of their archetypal meaning, and study of the archetypes is desirable for anyone interested in Jungian dream interpretation.

THE TWO SYMBOLIC LEVELS

In dream interpretation, we have to be alert to both the mundane and the higher symbolic levels, and allow the dreamer him or herself ultimately to identify on which level a particular dream is operating.

MUNDANE SYMBOLIC LEVEL

Concrete and physical, and related on the one hand to basic self-preservation needs such as nutrition, bodily comfort and health, physical exercise, physical gratification and personal power; and to self-preservation emotions such as anger, fear, and the need to seek sympathy, nurturing and support from others. Also related to sexual needs such as erotic sensations, sensuality and sexual dominance or submission.

HIGHER SYMBOLIC LEVEL

More mental and abstract, and related to our urge to find meaning in life beyond self-preservation and sex. The motivation behind much creative activity, behind altruism and selflessness, and behind mystical and spiritual experiences.

47

COMPARING FREUDIAN AND JUNGIAN DREAM INTERPRETATIONS

A comparison between the dream interpretations of Sigmund Freud and Carl Jung provides us with examples of the different levels of dreaming (*see* box on p.47). Some dreams operate at what I term the *mundane symbolic level*, namely the level of Freud's self-preservation drives and sex drives, while others operate at what I term the *elevated symbolic level*, that is Jung's higher order level of psychological and spiritual understanding and growth.

It is revealing to look at examples of Freudian and Jungian interpretations respectively. I have deliberately chosen two dreams for the purpose that contain an identical theme – namely the death of the dreamer's mother.

FREUD'S DREAM INTERPRETATION

A young woman in therapy with Freud had the feeling that she didn't want to see any of her relatives again, as they 'must think me horrible'.

She then recalled a dream she had had when four years old of a lynx walking on the roof of her house, then of herself or something else falling down, then of her mother 'being carried dead out of the house'.

In the analysis of the above dream, Freud concluded it meant that as a child she had wished to see her mother dead, and that it was because of this repressed wish she now felt all her relatives hated her.

In further support of this interpretation, the young woman remembered that as a very young child she had been called 'lynx-eyed' as a term of abuse by another child, and that when she was three years old a tile had fallen off the roof, hitting her mother and making her head bleed profusely.

JUNG'S DREAM INTERPRETATION

In the example of Jung, the dreamer is again a young woman. In her dream she comes home late at night to find the house 'as quiet as death'. In the living room she sees her mother hanged from the chandelier, her body 'swinging to and fro' in the cold wind from the open window.

In the dream analysis, Jung concludes that 'mother' is being used by the dreaming mind as an archetypal symbol for the unconscious, and that the dream is therefore telling the dreamer that her unconscious life is destroying itself'. He also correctly predicted that it gave warning of grave physical illness.

These two examples do not indicate a necessary conflict between Freud and Jung over the meaning of the dream image 'mother'. Rather they show that in dream interpretation we must study this and all other images in context. In the case of Freud's patient, the association of 'lynx' with a term of abuse, plus the actual memory of a tile falling on the mother's head and causing injury, were sufficient to confirm Freud in his belief that the actual parent was the subject of the dream, and that the dream acted out the patient's repressed hostility towards her.

In the case of Jung's patient, there was no evidence of this kind, and the analysis thus looked for deeper meaning.

These two examples are presented here in very shortened form. In both cases the interpretation concerned would have involved much more detail that I have been able to give, and would have been set against the many other insights into the patients' lives that had emerged in the course of the therapist-patient interaction. But they show something of the complexity of dream interpretation, and of the vital importance of studying each dream on an individual basis rather than taking over interpretations ready made from dream dictionaries.

OTHER DREAMWORKERS

The belief that dreams use a complex symbolic language is central to the work of both Freud and Jung. Yet, is this belief accepted by all other psychologists involved in dreamwork? The answer is that they are accepted by many (particularly by those whose approach is psychodynamic) but not by all. Space allows us only two examples of psychologists who take a markedly different approach. The first accepts the symbolism of dreams but in a much more simplified form, while the second rejects symbolism altogether.

The first of these psychologists is Fritz Perls, the founder of gestalt therapy. For Perls, dream interpretation must start from the point that all characters and objects in the dream are in fact symbols, projections of ourselves and of the way we have been living our lives. Thus they are often parts of our personality that may currently be unacknowledged by our waking, conscious mind. The logic of this is that since we are each the authors of our own dreams, whatever we put into them must first of all be within us.

Perls, therefore, differed from Freud and Jung in arguing firstly that dream symbolism is the personal creation of each of us rather than part of a universal symbolic language, and secondly that it should be seen as connected with our life experiences to date rather than with innate instinctive drives.

In Perls' view, dreams for the most part represent unfinished emotional business carried over from these life experiences, and the therapeutic use of dreams, therefore, consists of getting at the personal emotional nuances that lie behind the dream imagery. To do this, Perls developed his role-play exercises, where the dreamer is called upon to speak out in turn for each of the significant characters or objects in his or her dream.

This approach shows another important break from Freudian or Jungian dream interpretations in that the dreamer does his or her own interpretation, in terms of his or her own symbolic language. The therapist may of course make suggestions, and if the work is being carried out in a group (another of Perls's departures from conventional dreamwork), other members of the group can also make contributions. But essentially the dream is the property of the dreamer, and he or she must never have meaning imposed upon it from outside.

The second example of a psychologist who rejected Freudian and Jungian dream symbolism is Medard Boss, who was among the founders of existential psychology, a psychology based upon the belief that each of us chooses what we wish to be and expresses our choice in every aspect of our behaviour. Boss broke with the centuries-old tradition that dreams always carry a manifest and a latent content, and developed instead a method that allowed the dream to tell its own story.

The dream interpreter should therefore have the ability, apparently simple but in reality hard to come by, of seeing clearly and accurately what is there before his or her eyes. Using this clarity and accuracy, Boss argued, most dreams reveal very quickly the dreamer's existential condition, bringing it home to him or her, often with shattering impact.

An example of the way in which Boss demonstrated his theory was to hypnotise five women – three healthy and two neurotic – and to suggest to them they should each dream about a man known to be in love with them, experiencing him naked, sexually aroused, and advancing towards them with clear sexual intent.

Boss's women dutifully dreamt of their respective male friends. The three healthy women enjoyed the dream enormously, dreaming of the scenario exactly as suggested by Boss and relating it to him with considerable gusto. The two neurotic women, however, missed the fun, and produced very anxious and unarousing versions. In one case the dream was not overtly of the lover at all but of a uniformed soldier advancing with a handgun, in the course of playing with which he nearly shot her, frightening her into waking.

If we examine these dreams we see that in the case of the three healthy women the dreams had no obviously disguised content. They were certainly wish-fulfilments, but far from being of repressed

DREAM INTERPRETATIONS BY PERLS AND BOSS

Perls's method of dream interpretation involved a great deal of verbal interaction between himself (together with members of the dream workshop) and the person recounting a dream, together with much acting out of the various elements in the dream. Attention was also paid to the dreamer's physical posture, since this reflected something of the emotions he or she had felt while dreaming, together with elements of his or her present emotional state. So it isn't easy to give a proper account of a Perls's workshop in a short space. But the following example gives something of the flavour.

The dream is of a lake drying up; the dreamer is concerned about this, but consoles herself with the thought that there will be treasure on the lake bed. But when the water has disappeared all she discovers is an old licence plate. Asked by Perls to play the role of the licence plate she comes up with 'I am no use because I'm of no value... outdated... I don't like being a licence plate... the use of a licence plate is to give a car permission to go... I can't give anyone permission to do anything because I'm outdated.' Asked to play the lake she says 'I'm drying up... disappearing... soaking into the earth... so maybe I water the surrounding area... new life... can grow from me.'

The interpretation that emerges is that nature doesn't need a licence plate (an artifical artefact) to grow – the dreamer doesn't have to be useless or to need permission to be creative, provided she allows herself to be involved in life.

Now here is an example of an analysis by Boss. The dream is of being far above the Earth and seeing a nuclear war about to break out between the great powers. No living people represent these great powers, only blocks of stone or chess pieces. A nuclear bomb falls into the sea, and the dreamer knows that something, perhaps a big fish down in the depths, has the power to explode it.

Discussing his dream, the dreamer wonders if the Earth symbolizes his personality, and the great powers his own embattled mental abilities. Boss rejects this. The dream means what it says. The dreamer's relationship to the world and everything in it is a distant one. He has reduced people to the status of inanimate objects or of chessmen. He is worried about the possibility of world catastrophe, but does nothing about it, remaining a passive observer. The one living element in the dream world (the fish) is hidden and is just as threatening to the dreamer as the blocks of stone and the chessmen.

The dream shows clearly that the dreamer is a self-isolated frightened man who has lost his footing in the world. There is nothing to be gained by trying to read any other kind of meaning into it.

unacknowledged material, they openly reflected the dreamer's conscious desires. 'Ah!' a Freudian would argue, 'but perhaps the dreamer simply used the naked lover as a symbol for much deeper material. Maybe he stood for her desire to have intercourse with some other male. Perhaps he symbolized her incestuous love for her father. Perhaps he symbolized something to do with power and dominance. And what about the dreams of the two neurotic women? Surely the handgun was a symbol for her unacknowledged feelings towards her lover's penis, while being nearly shot by it symbolized ejaculation or indeed even attempted intercourse?'

Boss would answer that in the case of the healthy women we need look no further than the dream at its face value. Nothing is gained by trying to read symbolism into it. And even in the case of the neurotic dream about a gun, surely the correct procedure is simply to see it as revealing the narrow, fear-drenched world of the dreamer. Such a world has no place for a sexually aroused and arousing lover. Within it, men are seen as intrusive and dangerous, and as uniform and faceless in their menace. Nothing is to be gained by seeing the gun as symbolizing a penis instead of simply as itself, an object of her fear and revulsion. In fact, in both dreams, any attempt at symbolic interpretation is actually counter-productive, since it detracts from the emotional impact of the dreams themselves. And the emotional impact is what carries much of the dream message.

SYMBOLIC VERSUS NON-SYMBOLIC DREAM INTERPRETATION

The symbolic and non-symbolic approaches are not necessarily as contradictory as at first appears. Both have their uses. We must be a little careful about how much we read into the results of Boss's work with his five women subjects, since their dreams sprang from his hypnotic suggestions rather than from their own unconsciousness. But assuming the women reported the dreams correctly (the hypnotised mind is notoriously inclined to create fantasies that afterwards are taken for realities), the results certainly show that people can dream about things purely at face value.

Or that they can dream about them at face value *at one level*. For let me emphasize here the vital point, overlooked by many psychologists but that we must understand if we are successfully to work with dreams, namely that like many of the events of waking life, dreams can *carry multiple meaning*. In the case of Boss's three psychologically healthy women, the dream events may therefore indeed have disguised other, deeper levels of meaning.

So the Freudian argument that the aroused lover could have symbolized some aspect of the subject's unconscious mind can certainly have truth in it. For example, as in Perls's approach, he could have symbolized the perhaps unrecognized masculine side of the subject's own nature. And in the case of the two neurotic women, something could in fact be gained by exploring whether the gun served in the dream as a symbol of the penis. For it might be that the subject was not frightened of all aspects of masculinity but only of male sexuality, and it would be important to know this. Equally importantly, something could be gained by exploring the image of the soldier 'playing' with his own gun and causing it to go off. There are possible symbols here for auto-eroticism, and the fact that the dreamer was nearly shot as result of this 'play' may indicate a deep-seated fear and guilt of such eroticism in herself.

These are speculations. But only a more open form of dream interpretation, which worked with the subject and her dream at both face and symbolic levels, could tease out whether these deeper levels were operating or not. Certainly dreams *can* work symbolically, and I present plenty of evidence to show this throughout the book. By concentrating only at face value, important symbolic meanings may therefore be overlooked. But this doesn't mean that dreams cannot carry a straightforward meaning too, and we must take care that in our search for symbols we don't overlook this level of interpretation.

55

The presence of this straightforward meaning indicated that we have to add another level to the two already identified, and I call this the *non-symbolic* or *face-value* level. It is convenient to number the levels as follows, though this numbering doesn't necessarily represent the existence of a rigid hierarchy between them:

- Level One: Non-Symbolic Level
- Level Two: Mundane Symbolic Level
- Level Three: Higher Symbolic Level.

AT WHICH LEVEL SHOULD WE WORK IN DREAM INTERPRETATION?

We may never be able fully to unravel the mystery of dreams, since there are no precise instruments available for exploring the deeper levels of the human mind. In their absence, we have to be guided by what is helpful. If a particular level of interpretation helps people towards a fuller understanding and a more effective reshaping of their lives, then in an acceptable sense that interpretation is 'true'. This is not as imprecise an approach as it may seem. Even in the most rigorously orthodox scientific theories, the acid test is still one of usefulness. It was Jung who, in psychology and in life generally, equated usefulness with truth. And since no scientific theory can be anything more than a human-made model of reality, to be 'believed' until it is superseded by something more useful still, the equation of dream truth with usefulness isn't badly out of step with what happens in other areas of human thinking.

OTHER CULTURES, OTHER APPROACHES

Before we leave this examination of different approaches to dreamwork, something must be said about the approaches of other, non-Western cultures.

For the Senoi people in the mountain jungles of Malaysia, dreams provide a somewhat similar function, although the emphasis is more upon transforming the dream experience in positive and pleasurable directions while it is actually taking place. Although not described in such terms by the Senoi, their dreamwork is directed towards emotional health. If you are menaced by danger in dreams, turn and confront it. If you are offered pleasure, go towards it. If someone tries to teach you something, listen to them. Working on one's dream emotions in this way is thought to help one's emotoions in waking life. Instead of one-way traffic, with the emotional experiences of our waking lives affecting the emotional content of dreams, traffic can flow the other way too, and the emotional content of dreams can affect the emotional experiences of our waking lives. Learning fearlessness in dreams thus helps us to be fearless in waking life, spontaneous acceptance of pleasure helps us to be spontaneous, listening to wisdom helps us to be wise.

NATIVE AMERICAN DREAMING

For the Native American, dreams were a way of telling the future, of managing psychological problems, and – most importantly of all – of contacting supernatural beings and obtaining power from them. Different tribes had different methods for inducing, interpreting and using dreams, but fairly common to them all was a strong belief in motivation, in the strength of will of the dreamer. If you wished for a particular kind of dream, offering you particular kinds of help and guidance, and concentrated upon it for a sufficient period of time, then it would eventually be given to you. Fasting, prayer, meditation and retreating to an isolated spot were all helpful. Sometimes in the dream, the dreamer would meet a spirit helper, who would remain with him, reappearing regularly in dreams, for as long as was needed. Sometimes the dreamer would learn a song in a dream, or a special skill, such as understanding the ways of animals. Sometimes, particularly if one aspired to becoming a shaman, one would wander among the spirits of the dead and learn secrets from them. Or one would take part in single-handed combat, or be torn apart by savage creatures and undergo a ritual death, only to be reassembled and reborn into a new personality. The dream would serve as an initiation into new ways of being, a transformation into a new and magical reality.

LEFT NATIVE AMERICANS USE DREAMS TO CONTACT THE SUPERNATURAL.

This belief sounds strange to many Western psychologists but actually there is no reason why it should. We know that dream emotions can influence our waking feelings. A bad dream can leave us upset for days, a good dream can leave us filled with joy. Since dreams are so intimately connected with our emotions at deep and fundamental levels, there is no rational reason why the emotional lessons we learn in them shouldn't have a permanent effect upon the way we feel about and react to life.

Finally, a word about dreaming in the great spiritual traditions of the East. In these traditions it is also taken for granted that you can work upon and gain control of your dream life, in this case primarily for the purposes of spiritual development. For example, it is claimed that the teacher can appear to the pupil in dream life (and vice versa), and that the following morning both will know that the visit has taken place and will agree on what has been said. More strikingly still, it is claimed that the dreamer can remain conscious throughout his or her dreaming, and that the height of achievement is when consciousness persists through sleep, flowing uninterruptedly through the waking hours, through dreaming sleep and through dreamless sleep.

Advanced practitioners also teach that slipping from wakefulness into sleep is a dress rehearsal for death, a dress rehearsal through which we each of us go every night. If we can learn to make proper use of this dress rehearsal by keeping our consciousness continuous, this teaches us how to die.

CREATIVITY, INTELLIGENCE AND DREAMING

CHAPTER THREE

Creativity, like dreaming, relies heavily upon the unconscious. Notice how, in creative activity, you may work on an idea or a problem until you get stuck, then dismiss it from your conscious mind only to find that some time later (the following morning perhaps, or days, weeks, even years afterwards) the development of the idea or the solution to the problem pops into your mind ready-made. Many great writers and scientists over the centuries have reported this phenomenon. It seems that the unconscious mind goes on working on the problem even though consciously you have forgotten all about it. The unconscious tries one possible solution after another until suddenly it recognizes it has hit upon something that might be helpful, and then pushes it up into your conscious mind for you to have a look at. We can call it, if we like, the 'Eureka' phenomenon.

In my own writing, if I'm faced with a sentence or a paragraph that won't come out right, the best strategy is to get up from my desk, make myself a cup of tea or coffee or take a stroll around the garden thinking of anything but my literary endeavours. When I return to my desk a few minutes later, the sentence or paragraph usually comes to mind without further problem. It's surely the most painless way of arriving at a solution imaginable. My unconscious does the work for me, and very grateful I am to it.

In much the same way, our unconscious does the work for us in our dreams. It creates them without our conscious help. We are simply the fascinated (or reluctant) actors in a ready-made script. As in the creative act in waking life, the unconscious functions independently of our conscious thinking, bringing us adventures and ideas that carry the same shock of surprise as if they were written by a total stranger.

Creativity in waking life and creativity in dreams are alike also in that the representations of reality they produce can be equally realistic and vivid. Through his or her creative imagination, the creative artist can produce detailed landscapes, human and animal faces, a world as lifelike as the view from our own windows, or a world so strange and evocative it can open a new dimension in our experience. So too does the artist who illustrates our dreams. Even people who claim they are incapable of visualization in waking life nevertheless see in their dreams a world so recognizable that it engages them as closely as does their daytime experience, and can linger as long in the mind to disturb and excite.

Another similarity is that in both creativity and dreams we often have little or no idea of the outcome. Novelists talk of the characters in their novels 'taking over' and deciding the rest of the plot for themselves. Painters talk of experimenting with shapes and colours until suddenly images leap into life. Musicians start with simple musical themes and end with major symphonies. Children build fantasy play-time worlds that dissolve and change like the enchanted kingdoms of fairy tales.

LEFT PAINTERS, PERHAPS MORE THAN ANY OTHER ARTISTS, USE THE LANGUAGE OF THE UNCONSCIOUS. THEY SPEAK OF IMAGES LEAPING TO LIFE FROM THEIR EXPERIMENTATION WITH COLOURS AND SHAPES.

Just so in dreams are we taken into the unknown. Our unconscious decides on the setting of the dream, on the characters, on the plot, on the ending. Or sometimes on the absence of an ending, for if it chooses it can stop the dream tantalisingly in mid-story, like a film breaking down, leaving our conscious mind ever afterwards to ponder on what might have been.

ABOVE THE CHARACTERS AND STORYLINE OF OUR DREAMS FIND FORM IN OUR UNCONSCIOUS.

61

Yet another similarity is the way in which both creative experiences in waking life and experiences in dreams have the ability to engage us emotionally as deeply as the most moving of real-life events. We cry over stories, and we awake crying over dreams. Stories terrify us, enrich us, amuse us, excite us, intrigue us. So it is with dreams. Poetry, music, paintings, sculpture stir our humanity into a recognition of the numinous and the divine. So it is with dreams. In defiance of all logic, these simulations of reality at times outdistance even reality itself, and may even call into question where reality really resides, in waking life or in dreams. As it did for example with the third century BC Chinese sage, Chuany-Tzu, who tells us: 'One night I dreamt I was a butterfly . . . Who am I in reality? A butterfuly dreaming I am Chuang-Tzu or Chuang-Tzu imagining that he was a butterfly?'

Finally, both creativity and dreams satisfy some deep urge that lies inside the human spirit. We never leave the world as we find it. The urge to transform it, to reproduce it in other shapes and in other materials, seems innate in us. We see this urge in children's play, in many of our recreational activities, even in the doodles we make on scraps of paper during dull meetings. But we see it particularly in art, in science and in dreams. Our human spirit has a restlessness about it, a constant questing and seeking, a desire to search beyond the mundane and familiar, to look into the distance and see what it can find. To take a piece of wood and turn it into a boat or a musical instrument or the image of a god. To invest the life around it with a life of its own making. Creative people are rarely happy unless they are creating. Even self-confessed uncreative people find many of their psychological problems vanish in the face of therapies that unlock their creative powers. Humans, in a very real sense, are born to create, and without this creativity, humans cannot venture into those splendid upper rooms of their personality of which I spoke earlier.

So dreams are there in part to satisfy this creative urge. To provide it with heightened inspiration in creative people, to keep it from fading altogether in the less creative. To deny our creativity is to deny part of our life, and to deny our dreaming is to deny a tributary of the splendid river through which our creativity flows.

CREATIVITY IN DREAMS

A valuable way of looking more closely at the links between creativity and dreaming, and of exploring how dreaming can enhance our own creativity, is to look at examples of dream creativity in famous people. One of the best known is the strange dream that inspired Samuel Taylor Coleridge's poem, *Kubla Khan*. Coleridge was in poor health at the time, and after taking laudanum (a tincture of opium that was commonly prescribed in the 18th and 19th centuries), he dropped asleep while reading in a travel book the words 'Here the Kubla Khan commanded a palace to be built.' When he woke, the poem describing the building of Kubla Khan's pleasure dome was there, ready-made in his mind, and only needed to be written down. Unfortunately, before he had completed the task, Coleridge had a visitor. When he returned to his study an hour later the rest of the poem, in the infuriating habit of dreams, had disappeared. Try as he might, Coleridge could not recapture the dream, and *Kubla Khan* was destined to remain an evocative and beautiful fragment rather than the literary masterpiece it might well have become.

Robert Louis Stevenson was another writer who drew inspiration for his work from his dreams. In his memoirs he tells us that by working on his dreams – through the simple method of telling himself stories as he was going to sleep – he found that his 'little people' (as he called them) carried on the task for him during the night, setting forth tale after tale for him 'upon their lighted theatre'. One of Stevenson's most famous stories, *The Strange Case of Dr Jekyll and Mr Hyde*, was the result in part of this method, and Stevenson conceded generously that his 'little people' deserved credit for the bulk of his writing.

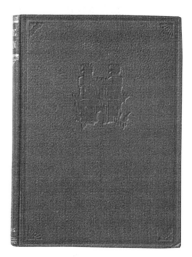

ABOVE DREAMS MAY GIVE US THE PLOT OF A NOVEL BUT WILL NOT NECESSARILY EDIT IT FOR US AS WELL.

63

William Blake is another literary figure who found inspiration in his dreams. Blake illustrated his poems with his own engravings, but the technique was expensive, and he found himself 'intensely thinking by day and dreaming by night' of how to come by a cheaper alternative. One night his dead brother Robert appeared to him in a dream and 'revealed the wished-for secret', namely a process of copper engraving.

Hearing music in dreams and then making use of it in their own compositions is by no means uncommon amongst musicians. One of the most celebrated examples is the 18th-century Italian composer Tartini, to whom the devil appeared in sleep and played a sonata on Tartini's own fiddle whose beauty, Tartini tells us, 'surpassed the wildest flights of my imagination'. Struggling unsuccessfully to recall it properly upon waking, Tartini nevertheless wrote the *Trillo del Diavola* (*The Devil's Trill*), which he considered the best work he had ever done.

Among the very many other creative men and women who claim their work was inspired at times by their dreams are Sir Walter Scott, John Keats, Charlotte Bronte, Mark Twain, Edgar Alan Poe, H. G. Wells, Katherine Mansfield, Graham Greene, J. B. Priestley, and Jack Kerouac. One can only guess at how many others have kept quiet about the same source of inspiration for fear of not having their work taken seriously.

Similarly, one can only guess at the number of people who have received inspiration in dreams and been unable to recall it in the morning. The belief expressed by some people that inspiration of this kind, no matter how world-shaking it seems to be in the dream itself, always turns out to be trivial if it is recalled is shown to be untrue by the examples I've just given. And here's a personal example of a short poem I dreamt recently and wrote down immediately on waking:

> *Come fly with me to Camden Town*
> *And I'll buy you a silken gown,*
> *Red roses for your shining hair,*
> *And velvet dreams beyond compare.*

There may be those who say such an example only goes to support the argument that what seems world-shaking in dreams turns out to be trivial on waking, but my reply is that I enjoyed the poem as much on waking as in dreaming. And I was pleased that it did manage to stay in my memory long enough to be recorded for posterity. A more telling example is the poem by writer A. C. Benson, a prolific recorder of dreams. Benson claimed that the poem (which he wrote down in the middle of the night immediately on waking) came without conscious volition, was in the style that in waking life he never attempted before or since, and consisted of symbolism that he could neither understand not interpret.

> *By feathers green across Casbeen,*
> *The pilgrims track the Phoenix flown,*
> *By gems he strewed in waste and wood*
> *And jewelled plumes at random thrown.*
>
> *Till wandering far, by moon and star,*
> *They stand beside the fruitful pyre,*
> *Whence breaking bright with sanguine light,*
> *The impulsive bird forgets his sire.*
>
> *Those ashes shine like ruby wine,*
> *Like bag of Tyrian murex spilt,*
> *The claw, the jowl of the flying fowl*
> *Are with the glorious anguish gilt.*
>
> *So rare the light, so rich the sight,*
> *Those pilgrims men, on profit bent,*
> *Drop hands and eyes and merchandise,*
> *And are with gazing most content.*

CAN DREAMS BEHAVE INTELLIGENTLY?

The artistic creativity exemplified in the last section is a form of problem solving. Deciding on the plot for a novel is, in its own way, just as much a problem as is how to split the atom. However, there are differences between the two types of problem. In the first instance, the solution to the plot of a novel is a divergent, open-ended one, with many possibilities and with no final right or wrong answers. By contrast, splitting the atom requires a focused solution, and is either correct or incorrect. This leads us to the question, can dreams show intelligent solutions as well as creative ones?

In many instances the two are called upon to work together, with creativity operating, so to speak, as the author, and intelligence as the editor. The author throws up a range of possible ideas, and the editor gets to work and decides which of them is most suitable for the purpose in hand. This is the case, for example, with certain scientific problems. There are many apparently possible ways to the solution, and the mind has to generate a range of them so that each in its turn can be put to the test until one is found that actually works.

There are many instances of scientists solving very precise problems in dreams, or obtaining such clear clues to them that the conscious mind was left with very little to do. One of the best known examples is that of the 19th-century German chemist Friedrich Kekulé, who claimed that his discovery of the molecular structure of benzene came to him in a dream.

The molecular structure of benzene is in the form of a chain of molecules arranged in the shape of a ring, and Kekulé describes his dream as showing him:

... the [molecules] gambolling before my eyes... frequently two smaller [ones] united to form a pair... a larger one embraced the smaller ones... still larger ones kept hold of three or four of the smaller, while the whole kept whirling in a giddy dance...My mental eye, rendered more acute by repeated visions of this kind could now distinguish larger structures of manifold confirmation; long rows, sometimes more closely fitted together; all twining and twisting in snakelike motion. But look! What was that? One of the snakes had seized hold of its own tail, and the form whirled mockingly before my eyes. As if by a flash of lightning, I awoke.

Thus the benzene ring, as it is called, presented itself to Kekulé in the form of a snake seizing hold of its own tail. But for Kekulé this snake symbolism was so clear that he grasped its meaning at once. For him, the solution given in the dream was a convergent one, and provides unequivocal evidence that dreams can indeed behave intelligently.

But in that case, why use symbolism at all? A ring isn't a difficult thing to show in a dream; people are dreaming about rings all the time. So why not dream about a ring made of molecules, especially since the dream presented the molecules themselves realistically enough? My answer is that for many dreams the unconscious deliberately chooses to use symbols. I mentioned earlier (see p.41 and p.43) that psycho-dynamic psychologists see the symbol as a protective mechanism, designed either to defend the conscious mind from the unconscious (as emphasized by Freud), or to avoid exposing it too abruptly to deep truths about ourselves (as emphasized by Jung). But there is a further explanation. Freud and Jung tell us only part of the story. It seems overwhelmingly that the unconscious uses symbolism in dreams because it actively wants to set us puzzles in order to stimulate us into inquiry. To prompt our conscious minds to start working creatively. To goad consciousness into keeping pace with unconsciousness.

In the great spiritual traditions of the East, the theme of humans being half asleep, unaware of who he or she is or of their destiny, is a constantly recurring one. *The Rubaiyat of Omar Khayyam* starts with the clarion call to 'Awake'!

> *Awake! for Morning in the Bowl of Night*
> *Has flung the Stone that puts the Stars to Flight:*
> *And Lo! the Hunter of the East has caught*
> *The Sultan's Turret in a Noose of Light.*

> *Dreaming when Dawn's Left Hand was in the Sky*
> *I heard a Voice within the Tavern cry,*
> *'Awake, my Little ones, and fill the Cup*
> *Before Life's Liquor in its Cup be dry.'*

OTHER EXAMPLES OF PROBLEM SOLVING IN DREAMS

In 1619 when he was 23, Descartes, one of the prime founders of modern scientific thinking, had three particularly vivid dreams in quick successsion one night that changed the whole course of his thinking. Already a gifted mathematician, Descartes was at the time turning to philosophy, and the three dreams involved a whirlwind, claps of thunder and two books, one a dictionary and the other a book of poems. Descartes, a devout Christian, believed that in the dreams God showed him the whirlwind to drive him forward, the thunderclaps as a sign the spirit of truth had descended upon him, and the books to reveal that poetry as well as philosophy had a part to pay in this truth. From these dreams came the illumination for what Descartes believed to be his greatest discovery, namely the unity of all the human sciences. Notice again the symbolism, in this case Biblical in content – the whirlwind, the thunder and the books.

One example of a discovery that helped establish modern science was that of the 19th-century Russian chemist Mendeleev, who after many fruitless attempts to tabulate the elements according to their atomic weights actually saw the required periodic table in a dream. Unlike the musicians and poets who struggle fruitlessly to recall dream inspiration, he remembered every detail of the table on waking, and wrote it down just as he saw it. Only one of the values later proved to need correction.

Mendeleev's dream is an example of non-symbolic dreaming. This is consistent with the point I made previously (*see* p.58) that the symbolism in dreams is a matter of choice. In Mendeleev's case it isn't easy to see how such an intricate table could be presented symbolically, so the unconscious apparently decided to give the information in undisguised form.

Another good example of problem solving in dreams is that of Hilprecht, a 19th-century expert on early Middle-Eastern civilizations. Hilprecht had been struggling all evening to decipher the inscriptions on two small fragments of agate, which were supposedly parts of Babylonian finger-rings, and of which he only had a rough sketch. Giving up the fruitless task, he went to bed and dreamt in remarkable detail that a priest of the Babylonian period appeared to him and explained that the fragments of agate came not from rings but from a votive cylinder (presented by King Kurigalzu to the temple), which he and his fellow-priests had cut into three parts in order to furnish adornments for a statue of the god Ninib. The priest informed Hilprecht that the two fragments in the sketch were the two parts that had gone to provide the god's earrings, but that no fragment of the third part would be found.

In the dream Hilprecht was told to put the two fragments together, which he did on waking. He was then able to read the following in translation from the rough sketch (allowing for certain missing letters): 'To the god Ninib, son of Bel, his Lord, has Kurigalzu, pontifex of Bel presented this.' Confirmation came later when Hilprecht examined the actual agate fragments themselves (which had been catalogued separately by the museum holding them, as no-one had realized their connection) and discovered that they fitted exactly together.

Another striking example comes from the German scientist Otto Loewi, who reported that the inspiration that led him to prove his theory of the chemical (as opposed solely to the electrical) transmission of nerve impulses came to him in a dream.

Other examples worthy of a mention are Agassiz, the leading Swiss naturalist who in 1848 reconstructed the zoological characteristics of a fossil fish that had long puzzled him and the German 18th-century acoustics expert Chladni, who claimed that his invention of the tuba was due to a dream in which the instrument appeared to him and caused him such excitement that he awoke as if from an electric shock.

PROBLEM SOLVING IN YOUR DREAMS

The main technique for opening oneself to the problem-solving abilities of the dreaming mind have long been recognized (though not, regrettably, by orthodox Western psychology).This technique is intended specifically for clear-cut problems that have a convergent, intelligent, single right answer.

1   Allow the waking mind to study the problem as much as it likes in its attempt to find a solution. Don't be too intense about it. As with most instances when we try to engage deeper levels of our mind, a curiosity-based, almost playful approach is better than a fierce, do-or-die one.

2   When it's finally clear that the solution is not coming, put the problem out of your conscious mind if you can, but in an optimistic, 'I know the solution is bound to come' frame-of-mind rather than a defeated one.

3   Each time the problem re-enters your mind, tell yourself confidently that you needn't bother with it now because you know you'll solve it later, during your dreams.

4   When you go to bed, hold the problem lightly in your mind, but making no attempt to solve it. Try to keep it there as you drift off to sleep.

5   On waking, write down at once any dream you can recall. Don't study it first to see if it has relevance to your problem, simply write it down, in as much detail as you can.

6   Once you've recorded everything you can from the night's adventures, identify all the major images that cropped up. Free associate to them by asking yourself what they suggest to you.

7   Return to this exercise whenever you can during the day. Keep your mind open and free of anxiety. If the solution doesn't come easily, tell yourself it doesn't matter because you'll have a clearer dream that night.

8   Be patient. Don't dismiss the exercise because the answer doesn't come the first night. And don't tell yourself that your message to your dreaming mind wasn't strong enough to get through. You may have dreamt the solution early in the night and forgotten the dream by morning. Or the solution may be there in your remembered dream, and so far you haven't teased it out. Tell yourself that it will be given to you more plainly tonight.

ABOVE KEEP A CAREFUL NOTE OF THE MAJOR THEMES AND IMAGES OF YOUR DREAMS. THEN USE THESE NOTES TO FREE ASSOCIATE.

If you don't have specific problems to work on, ask someone to give you a difficult anagram or a mathematical puzzle. Problems of this kind, where the right answer already exists and where you can keep checking your own solution against the original problem, provide excellent practice.

Once the technique starts to work for you, your dreaming mind should become more sensitive to real-life problems as well.

71

In the West we see the same theme in Jung's metaphor of the occupant of a splendid house never moving outside the basement.

It may seem strange that dreams could be there to help us wake up, when in ordinary thinking we use the term 'dreamer' precisely for the purpose of describing someone who is half asleep. But judging by the creative and intelligent 'leaps' that Kekulé and others are able to make in dreams this seems indeed to be the case; with symbolism, by its very other-worldly and intriguing nature, helping to make the dream memorable and to tease the receptive mind into effort and inquiry.

BETWEEN WAKING
AND SLEEPING

CHAPTER FOUR

At this point we need to look at the actual business of falling asleep if we are fully to explore our potential for making use of our dream lives. Although we are not certain as to the precise function of sleep, most people feel that during sleep their minds take a rest from the stress of waking life. This rest begins even before we actually sink into the first phase of our sleep cycle. In the moments between waking and sleeping, as we begin to lose touch with the world around us without yet showing the physiological changes of sleep itself, we go through a strange half-way house known as the hypnogogic state in which the mind presents us with a series of brief, hallucinatory images. In its most elusive, enchanted quality this state rivals dreaming itself, and for many practical purposes we can indeed treat it as a form of dreaming. Over the last two decades it has attracted increasing research attention in sleep laboratories, and we now have considerable evidence as to its nature.

LEFT THE MOMENTS BETWEEN SLEEPING AND WAKING HAVE

A PARTICULAR MAGICAL QUALITY OF THEIR OWN.

In the hypnogogic state, we experience not so much the story-making experience of the dream proper, though this can happen, as a succession of disconnected fleeting pictures, some of them possessing a curious vivid beauty. If you feel you have never experienced this state, recall a time when you were suddenly aroused just as you were dropping off to sleep. You will most probably remember you were in the middle of some particularly delightful thoughts, yet frustratingly were unable to recall exactly what they were. You maybe struggled to hold on to the last fragments of their memory, yet in the moment of grasping them, they finally and irrevocably eluded you.

There is a similar half-way house as we climb up each morning from sleeping to waking. Known this time as the hypnopompic state, it is characterized by the same vivid, disconnected images (though I for one am not alert enough in the mornings to be properly aware of them, and have to take their existence rather on trust). Research shows that the hypnogogic and the hypnopompic states are so much alike that there is probably no need to have two separate names for them. So from now on I shall refer only to the hypnogogic, and everything I say will apply equally to both of them.

HYPNOGOGIC IMAGERY

The intriguing thing about much hypnogogic imagery is its involuntary nature. One bright image follows another, without any apparent association between them, and without any obvious links to one's waking experiences. In my own case, for example, I may see a river flowing through a beautiful green landscape of hills and distant mountains, followed by a solitary man seen in profile sitting under a tree, followed by the rooftops of houses in a strange town, followed by boats on a canal and so on. None of these images relate to any place I've been or any picture I can remember seeing. One moment there is nothing there behind my closed eyelids, the next an image leaps up, ready made, as if setting the stage in a magic picture show.

I seem to 'see' the images with my left eye rather than with my right, which suggests a connection with the right hemisphere of the brain (see p.26). Sometimes the images are preceded by, though usually unconnected with, similar phenomena at the auditory level. That is, by verbalizations that, like snatches of overheard conversation, leap from nowhere into my mind. Mostly they deal with trivial matters that have nothing directly to do with me. A comment about the weather. A description of a place. But they come with a clarity comparable to that of the visual experiences, and seem to arise from the same source. For some people there can also be bodily sensations at this time, such as a feeling of floating or flying, and sometimes the body gives a sudden jerk, as if falling, which often seems to be in direct response to one or other of the visual or auditory experiences.

The visual and auditory hypnogogic experiences are similar to those that sometimes arise in meditation, suggesting that the mind briefly touches similar levels in both conditions.

Meditators, as well as those interested in dreams, sometimes ask whether there are techniques that can make us more aware of such experiences and help us further develop their richness. The answer is that yes there are, and that such techniques are a valuable lead-in to the use and control of dreams themselves.

74

ABOVE MEDITATORS OFTEN EXPERIENCE SIMILAR IMAGES TO THOSE
THAT OCCUR DURING THE HYNOGOGIC STATE.

BECOMING AWARE OF
HYPNOGOGIC IMAGES

These techniques all depend upon something that sounds deceptively simple but can prove remarkably difficult, namely maintaining awareness into the hypnogogic state and watching what happens during it. When we go to bed most of us think for a few minutes about the events of the day until, lulled by the comfort of the bed and the relaxed state of the body, we allow sleep to take over. After the first few minutes, the process becomes an involuntary one – sleep comes of its own accord.

There is nothing wrong with any of this, and we shouldn't try every night to change these pleasant habits. Nevertheless, if we want to use our dreams, we need gradually to introduce some elements of control into the process of falling asleep. The essential element in gaining this control is to watch more closely the process as it unfolds. As this often leads to a prolonged period of wakefulness in the beginner, you should not try to do it every night – two or three times a week is enough. And when you attempt it, for goodness sake don't lie there in gritted determination, forcing yourself to be attentive come what may. This destroys the whole object of the exercise and hypnogogic images will never arise. What you are aiming to do is to drift off to sleep as usual, yet to allow part of your mind to watch the process unfold. This part of the mind is going to be overtaken by sleep just like all the rest, but not until the last moment.

So settle yourself for sleep, stop thinking about anything special, and allow a kind of relaxed alertness to remain. I find it particularly helpful to place my awareness behind my closed eyelids, as if I'm patiently watching for something to happen, but not minding too much if it doesn't. Other people like to place their awareness between and above the eyes, in the place of the 'third eye' of yoga. The heart region is another possibility, so is the crown of the head.

These last three positions are three of the chakra regions, the non-physical energy centres taught in yoga philosophy, and you can use any of the other such centres if you prefer. It is sometimes said that the kind of visions you have will depend upon which of them you choose. If you choose the lower chakras in the perineum and the abdomen you will have sensual visions, and if you choose the crown of the head you will have exalted ones. These are very much matters for personal exploration, but to begin with, the eyes themselves, or the 'third eye', are good places. The most vital thing, as in meditation, is simply to have a place upon which to focus the mind.

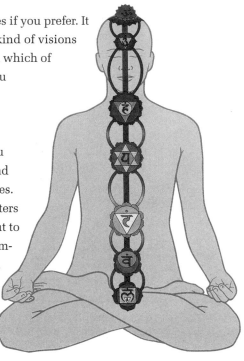

Let's assume you choose the eyes. Make sure that the eye muscles are perfectly **ABOVE** TO ACHIEVE A HYPNOGOGIC STATE, TRY TO FOCUS YOUR AWARENESS BEHIND ONE OF THE CHAKRA REGIONS.

relaxed, and just look into the darkness. The first few nights you try this, you'll probably drift off to sleep before anything happens. Don't be discouraged. Results may take a while to come, but this doesn't mean you're not going to get them.

Maybe the first time you try, maybe the second or the third, maybe the hundredth, you will suddenly become conscious of an image appearing. Never try to force it to do so. You can easily make yourself imagine something, but this is a conscious effort, just like our attempt to imagine something when fully awake. The point about a hypnogogic image is that it suddenly appears, ready made, like a fish leaping out of water. There is no mistaking the difference between it and something you put there consciously. At first the image may be very faint, so fleeting you might easily miss it. Don't expect something vivid and brightly-coloured right from the word 'go'. Or your first experience may be of words, like the overheard snatches of conversation I mentioned earlier. Whichever it is, don't try to hang on to it or prolong it. Don't think about it and start speculating as to what it might or might not mean. If you do, you'll lose it at once. Simply observe it. Don't get excited about it. See it and let it go, which it will do all too soon.

After a few of these images, you will probably drift off to sleep. Fine. There's nothing to be gained by deliberately trying to prolong the hypnogogic state. As like as not, all that will happen is that in your efforts to do so you will bring yourself fully awake, and once you wake from this state it is often very hard indeed to re-enter it and to go beyond it into sleep.

With practice, it becomes possible not only to observe the hynogogic state but to remember some of the images contained in it even when you wake the following morning. You may not necessarily remember all the details, but you will at least remember the settings. Don't, by the way, think that by observing the images you are somehow 'creating' this state. It happens anyway, every night. The only difference now is that instead of being too close to sleep to notice it, part of your mind is still aware.

The main value of working with the hypnogogic state is that it puts us progressively into closer touch with our unconscious. It is a way

BELOW IN THE HYPOGOGIC STATE, BOTH BRAIN AND BODY ACHIEVE HIGH LEVELS OF RELAXATION.

TECHNIQUES TO HELP YOU REACH A HYPNOGOGIC STATE

If you have trouble in establishing an awareness of the hypnogogic state, put more emphasis upon the point at which you are directing your awareness. Hypnogogic images can sometimes be induced in the waking state by the technique of scrying, that is by staring at a polished surface or into a bowl of water stained with black ink or into a crystal ball. In one of the Tibetan traditions, the teaching is to imagine a spinning disc of light at this awareness point (the heart chakra point is particularly recommended for this purpose). After visualizing this disc, images will start to flash through it. Just observe them, and in the intervals between them, return to your contemplation of the spinning disc.

Another technique is to keep the name of an object you would like to see at the centre of your awareness, gently and without effort. A red rose perhaps, or a broad river, or a snow-capped mountain. Don't try and 'create' the image for yourself. Simply think of it in an abstract way. When the image appears, it will often be different in detail from the one in your mind. The red rose might turn out to be a pink or yellow one, the broad river a rushing stream or a waterfall, the snow-capped mountain a green hill topped by a pine forest. Or a different image altogether might appear. Simply observe what happens.

A further suggestion is to practise observing numbers or the letters of the alphabet in sequence, in the colour of your choice and on a contrasting background (blue on white perhaps, gold on black, yellow on blue). This may prompt images that have to do with letters or numbers, but it can be a useful way of getting the practice established.

RIGHT THE IMAGE THAT APPEARS MAY
VARY FROM THE ONE IN YOUR MIND.

of beginning to explore some of those other rooms in our splendid mansion. Our unconscious throws up these images. Why? What do they mean to us? And why these particular images and not others? One view advanced by the orthodox theories on dreaming is that, as the onset of sleep makes us increasingly oblivious to the signals received from our senses, so the brain tries desperately to keep in touch with the outside world by inventing its own signs and sounds. Another is that the images are simply the result of our brain cells continuing to fire off their signals, in a haphazard way as we drop off to sleep. Rather like the way in which sometimes a car engine goes on firing for a moment or two after we switch off the ignition.

However, as with dreaming, anyone who takes the trouble to study this state for themselves quickly becomes aware of the poverty of this kind of explanation. Like dreams, the hypnogogic images are creative. They go beyond the information given. Rather than consisting merely of odd bits of form or colour put together randomly from the day's experiences, they present us with something new and coherent. We see breathtaking scenery that we have never seen before, we see people and images, we see events taking place.

In the hypnogogic state what we might call the 'filters' that operate when we are fully awake, and that prevent much of the material not directly relevant to our waking concerns from getting through into consciousness, are removed. If we doubt the creative power of these images, and their capacity for disturbing and engaging us, for filling us with a strange feeling that somehow we have visited all these places before, that we know what they mean, although we can't quite remember what this meaning is, look at Surrealistic art. The Surrealists were very influenced by their dreams, but perhaps even more by the hypnogogic visions. In their paintings we see echoes of these visions, strange enigmatic landscapes, the imposition of fantasy upon reality or of reality upon fantasy, an entry into another world that is frightening, hauntingly beautiful, enigmatic, and yet somehow familiar. Our own inner world, closer than the view from the bedroom window or than the four walls within which we sleep.

DEALING WITH UNPLEASANT IMAGES

Of course, like dreams themselves, not all hypnogogic images are pleasant ones. Sometimes you may see threatening faces or dark gloomy scenes. View them with the same sense of detached interest. Life itself presents us with unpleasant as well as pleasant scenes, and we cannot expect either in hypnogogy or in dreams always to escape the former. To be able to see the unpleasant images without fear or alarm is good practice. The Tibetans teach that they are similar to the wrathful deities that we see in the *bardo* (limbo) state after death, and that by confronting them instead of fleeing from them we enhance the control that we have over this state.

Research into the hypnogogic state shows that for many people even the most frightening images fail to produce an unpleasant reaction. Such people report they feel a surprising lack of emotional response to these images, either at the time or afterwards. They speak of a 'detached involvement'. They are drawn to the images, yet view them as if from a position beyond the normal world of petty anxieties and tensions. This leads some authorities on the hypnogogic state to argue that part of its purpose is to act as an anxiety-reducer. It's there to show us that we don't really have to be terrified by the pictures with which life presents us. We can look upon the most disturbing scenes with equanimity and without the feeling that we must escape from them. And we can survey the most beautiful ones with serenity and without the feeling that we must grasp and hold onto them.

Should the unpleasant images prove particularly persistent however, don't make the mistake of trying too hard to push them away. This only communicates to the unconscious the fact that they have strong negative significance for you and, in the perverse way with which the unconscious deals with such matters, succeeds in strengthening them. The technique for banishing them is to focus upon something that is abstract and as unlike them as possible. Try for example a geometric shape, preferably in the form of a mandala, that has positive associations for you. Don't consciously attempt to construct the shape for yourself. Keep the mind in its detached state, and simply suggest to it what you want to see, and then wait for it to emerge.

ABOVE TO GET RID OF NEGATIVE OR FRIGHTENING IMAGES, TRY TO VISUALIZE AN ABSTRACT SHAPE SUCH AS A MANDALA.

But, helpful as working upon the hypnogogic state undoubtedly is as a preliminary to understanding and using your dreams, it isn't essential. If the negative hypnogogic images persist and become frightening, it's better to give this state a miss for the time being. You can return to it later, when you have gained more understanding of your dream life.

81

YOUR DREAMS AND THEIR MEANING

CHAPTER FIVE

We have now reached the point where we can start interpreting our own dreams. If you've been working on remembering your dreams and have started keeping a dream diary, you should also have some useful material with which to start. It is perfectly possible – and often desirable – to interpret individual dreams, but if you have several to look at this is even better. Often you can identify patterns and recurring themes across them, and these indicate that your unconscious has particular preoccupations that need careful investigation.

In chapter 2, I looked at the many ways in which dreams have been interpreted across the centuries, and paid particular attention to four modern Western psychological approaches, those of Freud, Jung, Perls and Boss. Between them, these four approaches give a comprehensive picture of the way in which our dreams can be encouraged to yield up their meaning. We do not have to choose one particular approach but can use a combination of the four in our own work. Remember that I said that dreams operate on a number of different levels. This means that any approach to dreaming that sticks rigidly to just one level cannot give us a full picture and complete understanding, and if applied dogmatically can even mislead us altogether.

DREAM SYMBOLISM

The world is full of symbols. A symbol is simply something that stands for something else. Words themselves are symbols, and so are numbers. Most of the time we use symbols denotively, that is to say they convey something definite – the word 'dog' stands for the animal dog, the number '100' stands for a specific quantity. However, symbols can also be used metaphorically. The word 'dog' can stand also for a person of bad behaviour, the number '100' can also stand for a landmark in a batsman's innings or a snooker player's visit to the table. Metaphorical symbols carry a complex of meanings and attitudes usually at a subjective mental level, and it is metaphorical symbols that interest us in dreams.

The reason for this interest is precisely because they represent such a complex of meanings and attitudes, some of which we are well aware of at the conscious waking level, but others of which lie unacknowledged in the unconscious. Unlocking the hidden meaning behind these symbols therefore gives us an insight into the unconscious.

Metaphorical symbols may be personal to ourselves (a particular design of armchair may symbolize old age for you because your grandmother always sat in one), or we may share them with most of our fellow human beings. For example, 'high' is a universal symbol for success, 'low' for failure. It is these shared symbols that are of particular interest. Jung sees them as giving access to the collective unconscious (*see* chapter Two).

RIGHT THE WORD 'DOG' CAN BE DENOTATIVE AS HERE BUT IT MAY ALSO HAVE A SYMBOLIC MEANING.

WORKING WITH DREAM SYMBOLS

There are two major ways of working with dream symbols. The first is to study your dream diary for their appearance. Take for example the symbols known as archetypes (see pp.44–47). Jung tells us that among the most important in dreams are the shadow (our own dark side, represented by an enigmatic or hostile person), the child (primordial innocence and wisdom), the hero (our ideal self), the wise old man (acquired wisdom), the mother (creativity, the unconscious) and the maiden (beauty, truth). But archetypes can also be in the form of things not experienced in waking life such as dragons, helpful animals, gods, hidden treasure, strange masks and alchemical processes. Archetypal situations also exist, such as flying through space, becoming the sun, moon or earth, dying or becoming a stranger to oneself. Archetypal dreams are Level Three dreams, and Jung claims they can always be recognized by their cosmic, deeply significant feeling.

The second way is to choose a particular symbol as a focus for meditation then watch for its appearance in your dreams. Look at a picture of it or visualize it. The mandalas used in Eastern religions are ideal, as are alchemical symbols. So is the Celtic cross, or the geometrical shapes I suggested you use in the hypnogogic state (*see* p.78).

Stick to the same symbol. Frequent change hinders progress.

LEFT THE CELTIC CROSS IS A USEFUL IMAGE TO FOCUS ON DURING MEDITATION. IN TIME, THIS IMAGE, OR ANY OTHER THAT YOU HAVE CHOSEN, SHOULD SURFACE IN YOUR DREAMS.

84

The three levels I identified are:

Level One: The Non-Symbolic Level

Level Two: The Mundane Symbolic Level

Level Three: The Higher Symbolic Level.

Of these levels, Level Three dreams are the rarest, and can be recognized by the great impression they make upon us both at the time and after waking. Often these dreams stay undimmed in the mind for years, and may leave you with feelings of great peace and tranquillity (or with feelings that they represent some kind of unfinished business that you must at all costs come to understand and resolve). Jung called them 'great dreams', and identified them as invariably carrying archetypal images (*see* box opposite).

Once you begin to work on your dreams, these dreams may become more frequent.

In the same way there are marked individual variations between the relative frequency with which we each of us experience Level One and Level Two dreams. Some people have a preponderance of Level One dreams, others of Level Two. However, we should make judgements about this, seeing for example anyone who has frequent Level Two dreams as being more psychologically or spiritually 'advanced' than the person whose dreaming takes place mainly at Level One.

SINGLE AND MULTI-LEVEL DREAMS

Some dreams work at only one of the levels, others may contain elements of all three. Dreams operate intelligently and creatively, and they can introduce a particular image and then proceed to use it at all three levels. In your dreamwork, therefore, do not necessarily stick at a single interpretation. Go on working with the dream image to see if it carries further meaning. On the other hand, don't feel that an image must carry more than one interpretation. If one interpretation feels right, and nothing else comes up, then the chances are there is only one level of meaning with which to concern yourself.

ABOVE WITH PRACTICE, YOU WILL BE ABLE TO INTERPRET YOUR DREAMS WITH HONESTY AND CONVICTION.

In all work of this kind, the golden rule is that the interpretation must feel right to you. However, this does not mean you are free to manipulate it until it tells you what you want to hear – be totally honest with yourself. However, it usually means that if an interpretation doesn't seem relevant to your life situation, then it probably isn't the right one.

Remember that dreams are a product of the unconscious, so they don't have to carry their meaning in the logical, rational way of the conscious mind. So when interpreting them, put your mind into a free-wheeling, playful mode, simply allowing whatever wants to emerge from the unconscious, however outlandish, to do so. It may be rubbish or it may not be. Take everything at its face value, until you've got a number of responses to the dream and can then begin to examine each one more closely.

Remember also that in work of this kind you must be patient. The dream may not reveal its meaning at first go. If it doesn't, keep it in your mind over the following days. Return to your dream in your thoughts whenever you can, not with a grim 'I will solve it' mentality, but in an open, intrigued, curious frame of mind – 'What does it mean I wonder?'

Since dreams are a product of our creativity, enlist your other creative powers to help your interpretation. Draw or paint your dreams. If you enjoy music make up a tune that seems to represent the dream. If you like words, write a line or two of poetry. Try modelling the significant dream images in clay. Speak to the dream.

STEPS IN DREAM INTERPRETATION

When you are ready to start dream interpretation, study your
dream diary and make notes of:
• Recurring dreams. Some people dream largely the same dream
either on several consecutive nights or at regular intervals over a
longer period.
• Recurring images and themes. Look for the same people cropping
up in dreams (are they strangers or people who are known to you?,
what role are they taking?), or the same kind of situations, or the
same emotions.
• Dream events that make a particular impact (happy, frightening,
puzzling) on you; also dream characters.
• The feelings and thoughts that your dreams leave you on
waking, even if these have no obvious connection with the
dreams themselves.
• The quality of your dreams. Are they diverse and interesting?
Exciting? Dull? Menacing? Long? Short? Coherent? Disconnected?
Erotic? Embarrassing?
• The dream scenery. Is it of familiar or unfamiliar places? Town or
country? Are there dominant colours? Are they bright or dark?
Write all these things down,
preferably in your dream diary
immediately underneath the
account of the dream itself. Have
them in front of you when you start
your interpretation. It may be
helpful to draw up a table, with
dream images and events listed
down the left, and the frequency
with which each occurs entered
in columns.

ABOVE DOES THE SCENERY OF YOUR
DREAMS APPEAR FAMILIAR TO YOU?

87

Ask it directly what it means. If the answer doesn't emerge, ask it to make its meaning clearer in the dreams you're going to have tonight. Although dreams seem to like to set us puzzles, there's no reason for thinking they want the answer to remain forever obscure. Dreams can hardly help us towards wholeness, to put our unconscious and our conscious minds in communication with each other, if all they want to do is baffle and confuse.

LEVEL ONE INTERPRETATION

Once you have gone through your dream diary or your individual dream in the way suggested in the box (*see* p.87), pick out those themes and aspects that occur with particular frequency and/or that seem to you to be significant. Work on them first of all at Level One. Do they have meaning for you at face value? Perhaps these significant dream happenings tell you something about the world and how you see it. Are they:

- Optimistic or pessimistic?
- Indicative of a broad or narrow life?
- Confident or fearful, sure or unsure?
- Evidence for individuality or conventionality?
- Colourful or drab?
- Orientated towards male or female images and events?
- Peaceful or violent?

And so on. Work on the assumption your dreams are trying to tell you something. Even if your life is happy and successful, there will be things about it that could usefully be changed – emotions you are repressing or denying, ambitions or goals from which you have perhaps wrongly turned away. Don't expect your dreams always to dwell on the light and positive side of life. Don't be afraid of what they have to tell you. For example, as I shall show in due course, even a pattern of violent dream images doesn't mean you are a violent person (nor does a pattern of erotic dreams mean you're over-sexed!).

Because we describe Level One dreaming as non-symbolic, this doesn't mean that everything at this level simply features things as they are in real life. Even at Level One, the dream is a dramatization. But at this level the meaning is straightforward and clear, and doesn't require symbolic interpretation.

ABOVE DREAMING OF MONEY MAY SIMPLY MEAN YOU HAVE FINANCIAL PROBLEMS OF SOME KIND.

When you've looked at what the dreams may be telling you about the general pattern of your life, look more closely at some of the individual dream happenings. With each one, think of it as simply being what it seems to be. If you dream of losing a sum of money for example, this may show you have a specific anxiety about financial loss, or a more general fear about losing the things you value. Try this interpretation and see if it fits. If you have a dream about success, this may show you prize success or are anxious to achieve success. Again try obvious non-symbolic interpretations like this and see if they fit.

Work on your dreams at Level One until you feel you have identified all they have to say to you at this non-symbolic level. Then go on to Level Two.

LEVEL TWO INTERPRETATION

I've already said that some dreams may reveal all their meaning at Level One. So don't feel they have to carry a symbolic meaning as well. Just explore them to see. If after a while nothing of value emerges, leave it at that. Go back to Level One Interpretation, and see if there are any further areas of non-symbolic meaning that remain to be explored.

89

In working at Level Two, the respective methods of Freud, Jung and Perls are all relevant. All three, in their rather different ways, produce legitimate results. So at first experiment with all three. If, as you develop your experience, or find that one of them produces better results for you than the other two, own it as your personal technique and use it in preference to the other two. Only revert to one or other of these if you reach a block when working on a particular dream. The change of technique usually gets you through the block.

FREE ASSOCIATION

The best method with which to start as a beginner is free association, since this is easy and (usually!) fun to use, and helps to open up the flow of creative, intuitive ideas so necessary in dreamwork. In order to free associate, take one of the significant aspects that emerges from your dream diary or from an individual dream – it may be a person, an event, a colour, a feeling, an object – and hold it in your mind. Play with it. Mentally turn it over and study it from every angle. Don't dissect it though. Keep it whole, just as it is.

What comes into your mind as a result? A picture? An idea? A word? Don't judge it or examine it or wonder why. Just hold it in your mind. What comes next? Another picture, another idea, another word? Hold that in your mind and see what it suggests. Now see what that suggests and so on.

Allow the mind to free-wheel, following this train of ideas. Don't interfere. Don't wonder why you should be getting so far away from the original dream image. Just follow the train until it arrives at something that seems significant to you or which carries a special emotional impact. It might be a sudden flash of awareness about yourself, a new insight into a problem, a memory from way back, a hidden emotion or attitude or prejudice about something or a new kind of understanding about some aspect of life itself.

Sometimes, instead of reaching this point, the associations just peter out. If this is the case you can return to the dream image and start again, or you can take another of your dream images and start from there, or you can regard this as a block, a defence mechanism that is preventing you from going any deeper, and to which you should return again and again until suddenly you break through and pick up the train of associations again. Only you can decide which of these three courses of action is appropriate, and you must decide on the strength of the intuitive feeling you have about it rather than upon any attempt at rationalization.

Let's take an example of free association in action. Starting with the image 'swing', one dreamworker came up with:

circle, round, grace, beauty, harmony, eternal, everlasting, globe, earth, world, kingdom, cabbala, mysticism, secrets, hidden, wonders, meaning, answer, rightness, justice, mercy, the foundation and kether, the crown.

Readers familiar with mysticism will recognize the cabbalistic symbolism here – kingdom, cabbala, justice, mercy, the foundation and kether, the crown – but the important thing for the dreamer is the way the associations reveal a concern with the higher nature of things. This concern may already be recognized in waking life. Free association often leads us back to what we already know, and re-emphasises for us its vital importance. Or it may be something that the dreamer has been trying to hide from himself. Either way, the train of associations leads to a significant point.

Free association works so well for most people, that you may wonder why we need to bother with the alternative approaches to dream interpretation of Jung and Perls. The answer is that although free association is a very powerful technique indeed for putting us in touch with ourselves, and for uncovering our concerns, our unconscious complexes, our psychological problems, our strengths and weaknesses, it may lead us away from the dream. In other words, it may tell us something very significant about ourselves, but this may not be the very significant something that the dream was trying to convey.

AMPLIFICATION

The Jungian approach tries to avoid this risk by using the powers of association in a rather different way. It gives more status to the dream by assuming that it is not really a disguise but means what it says – provided you can recognize what the symbols it uses are actually saying. Jung's method is a way of elaborating upon, or, as he called it, amplifying the dream image. Let's see how amplification works.

Select your dream image as in free association, and once more hold it in your mind just as before. Look at it from every angle. Now what comes into your mind? Look at this new image in turn, but don't allow it to spark off a train of associations that takes you away from the dream. Keep coming back to the dream. Keep the dream image in the centre of your awareness. Build up a constellation of associations around it, rather than a train of associations leading away from it.

For example, also starting from the dream image of a swing, but using amplification instead of free association, a dreamworker came up with the following:

child's plaything, garden, sunlight, swinging backwards and forwards in space, feelings of freedom and lightness, sounds of children's voices in the evening, my father pushing me on the swing, rising and falling, making progress then falling back, my father's safe hands always pushing me up again, enjoying going down as well as up, I can't go up without also going down, rising and falling are part of the same process, going down is as necessary in its way as going up, don't be discouraged by going down, falling is a prelude to rising, I must go on always, joyfully and freely.

See how these associations cluster around the idea of a swing and swinging. It is the swing that carries the message for the dreamer, telling him not to be discouraged by the inevitable setbacks to his progress in life. We can 'enjoy' – learn as much from the setbacks – as from the successes. If we learn from them in the right way, the former help us achieve the latter. Even in falling back there is security (the father's safe hands) provided we can see this always as part of life's lessons, the prelude to going forward once more.

However, no method of dream interpretation is perfect. Using only amplification, the dreamworker sometimes fails to make the intuitive leap between the symbol and its deeper levels of meaning. He or she becomes stuck, and needs to look at things from a new angle. Free association can provide this angle. Even if the free associations don't seem to lead you to your goal, the trail of images that they uncover is so rich that when you switch back to the original dream symbol again, new and more relevant amplifications spring into the mind, especially if you switch back suddenly, now.

ROLE PLAYING

The third of the methods, adapted from that of Perls, we can best think of as role playing. Identify the significant things in your dreams or dream just as before, but take particular care not to neglect anything. Working with this method, almost everything you remember about the dream may be significant (the same can of course be true when working with free association or with amplification). The very fact that a particular dream object is occupying a humble position in the dream, or is necessary to the dream action but hardly makes an appearance, may have something to tell you.

Once you have summoned up all the characters and events from the dream, see them as each in a sense representing a part of yourself. Take the role of each one in turn. What does it have to say to you? It's helpful to put two chairs facing each other, and move between them as you converse with these dream images. Working with the example given below – a dream about sitting in her office – a dreamworker talked with her desk in the following way:

DREAMWORKER: You're there every day. I sit at you from nine in the morning to five at night.
DESK: Yes, but you don't take much notice of me.

DREAMWORKER: Oh, I think I do. I notice you waiting for me in the morning. And I like to leave you tidy at ight.

DESK: That's not noticing me. That's just using me. You don't even know who I am.

DREAMWORKER: All right, who are you then?

DESK: You can't do without me. If you didn't have me you wouldn't be able to work.

DREAMWORKER: That isn't answering my question.

DESK (becoming suddenly angry): Who are you to be asking questions? Why don't you look at yourself for a change?

DREAMWORKER: What would I see?

DESK: A mess. You tidy me because you can't tidy yourself. I'm the only thing that keeps you going. You put all sorts of things on top of me. And then you think that just because you tidy me up at the end of the day everything is all right.

DREAMWORKER: Okay. So I'm the part of me that gets all the credit for being good at my job, and you're the part that really carries everything.

DESK: Sure. And you'd better take more care of me, or one day I'll collapse under the weight of it all.

Further work showed the dreamer that the desk was part of her inner resources to which she wasn't giving enough time and attention. It was the part of her that supported her work and her home and her family, the dependable part of her on which everyone relied. It was there and it was solid, and it was indeed dependable, the most dependable thing in fact in the frantically busy 'mess' of her life. But it needed a little time to itself. In the words of the desk, it needed dusting and polishing occasionally, it needed to be admired, to have its scratches touched up, to be protected from hot coffee cups and typewriter correcting fluid. It didn't want less attention than the mechanical things like the telephone and the tape recorder that it had to support.

In work of this kind, there is a risk of over-dramatization, of being carried away by the script instead of staying focused upon what the dream image is really trying to say. You become aware this is happening when the dialogue loses its emotional charge, and becomes simply wordy and clever. And the fact that you're taking the role of the dream image does mean that you shouldn't stray too far from it. As in Jungian dreamwork, constantly come back to the dream itself. For many people, role play is a highly effective way of getting into closer contact with the dream image, feeling it from the inside, so to speak, instead of only from the outside.

95

IMPORTANT CONSIDERATIONS AT LEVEL TWO

In working at Level Two, look particularly for wish fufilments when the dream shows you, usually in a disguised and exaggerated form, that there is repressed material or emotional drive in the unconscious that is seeking expression. Also look for compensations, when the dream makes up for some lack in the behaviour of your conscious self, and shows you that your personality lacks the necessary wholeness and balance.

LEVEL THREE INTERPRETATION

Level Three dreams may impress themselves upon us by that cosmic quality of which Jung speaks, but they may still need a lot of work before they reveal their full meaning. Unlike Level Two dreams, which may often use only symbols personal to the dreamer, Level Three dreams have a strong tendency to employ archetypal material (archetypes can operate at Level Two as well though, so their presence isn't an automatic indication you're now at Level Three). If you think you're working at Level Three, proceed as for Levels One and Two in your initial analysis of the dream content, but note particularly this archetypal material.

Once identified, don't assume the archetypes carry only their recognized archetypal meaning. Explore first any personal associations they may have, using free association, amplification or role play. Failure to do this may mean that you miss the message the archetype is trying to convey. For example, one woman dreamer dreamt that:

'I was being attacked by a savage dog, that first of all tried to bite me then began to call me names. I was rescued by a man who came out of the woods, and then the dog became friendly and started to lick my hand.'

LEFT FIERCE DOGS THAT SUDDENLY TURN FRIENDLY ARE COMMON ARCHETYPAL IMAGES IN LEVEL THREE DREAMS.

The dreamer's personal amplifications revealed a memory of having been frightened by a dog in a farmyard when she was young. This emphasized the child-like fears that were still part of her life. The archetypal figure of the talking dog that turns friendly then suggested to her that if she gives her hero side (her courageous side, symbolized by the archetypal hero figure who emerges from the concealment of the wood) a chance to reveal itself, it will tame the dog, which will then become her ally. The savage/tame dog then suggested to her the forceful, more aggressive side of her nature, which she had always been fearful of using in case it consumed the gentler qualities that she felt were the only things about her that other people prized.

Had she avoided the initial personal association and begun immediately to relate to the dog as a wise animal that had something to tell her, she might have missed identifying what that something actually was. Similarly she might have missed it if she had focused immediately on the hero archetype.

But however you approach them, some Level Three dreams don't reveal their meaning to you all at once. The meaning only becomes clear as your life events unfold, perhaps over the following months, even the years.

Don't be in too much of a hurry to grasp at this meaning. If you do, it could become hidden under a number of partial or even misleading interpretations, Instead, call the dream to mind from time to time, just like a memory from waking life. Recall its events in all the detail you can, including the feelings that they aroused. Go back to your dream diary to check these details, so that they don't become distorted. However, at the same time, don't 'fossilize' the dream. Regard its characters as living people, who may reappear in future dreams, and who are not bound just by the one adventure they shared with you.

Illustrate the dream (*see* p.86) as soon as you can after it happened, and keep the illustration in your dream diary. Often this will help you to recapture the flavour of the dream more fully than words on their own.

DREAM COMPLETION

Sometimes you experience a dream that remains maddeningly unfinished – it was just reaching a point where you felt something terribly momentous was going to happen, and then the dream ended or you woke up.

This can happen at all Levels, and with Level Three dreams you are left with a particular sense of loss. So try to resolve the dream for yourself. Put yourself as far as possible back into the atmosphere and the emotional feel of the dream, and let it play itself out.

Again patience is the key, together with a determination not to let the rational mind (or wishful thinking!) take over. The first time you try this, often nothing happens. The dream remains static. Like the freeze frame in a video, the action and everybody in it remain where the dream left them.

Resolve to try again in the future. Sometimes the completion, like an interpretation, seems to be waiting for certain real life events to take place before it becomes clear.

Sometimes it seems determined to remain forever enigmatic, not in order to be wilfully obscure but as a way of stimulating your creative thinking, of challenging you to go deeper and deeper into the unconscious.

Where you are able to complete a dream for yourself and the ending has that indefinable sense of rightness about it, enter it in your dream diary. But be sure to indicate in the diary that the ending was arrived at in this way. And be open to the fact that one day, out of the blue, a different ending may come to you. This doesn't mean your original ending was wrong. It's more likely a way of showing you that your life has moved on since then, with the alternative endings giving you some idea of the distance that has been travelled.

GROUP DREAMWORK

So far I've been assuming that, as with most people, you're working on your dreams on your own. But if you have a group of friends who share your interests in dreaming, you can work together. Let me repeat the general warning though that any interpretation arrived at must feel right to you. Don't accept the interpretations of the rest of the group, (or even a therapist), if they go aginst this feeling of 'rightness'. Suspect any interpretation that fails to strike an emotional chord, either positive or negative. Be honest and open with yourself, but in the end make up your own mind on whether they're appropriate or not.

I mention other people's interpretations because, human nature being what it is, other people will try and offer their opinions and solutions, no matter how hard they fight against the temptation. Ideally, a dream group should simply listen to your dream, and then help you with the process of exploring it, and not offer you their solutions. For example, they can suggest amplifications. They can even take the part of one of the characters in a role play exercise if you're badly stuck. And they can comment upon *your* amplifications and even upon your interpretation.

In group work of this kind, it's vital that the atmosphere is supportive, accepting, and non-judgmental. No-one is there to make anyone else feel inadequate, or to laugh at their dreams, or to criticize their attempts at interpretation. Sharing dreams, especially emotional or deeply felt ones, is only possible in the right atmosphere. Anyone who can't recognize this has no place in the group until they can. Also out of place is anyone who tries to monopolise proceedings, or to lay down the law as to what particular dream images mean (particularly if they brandish a dream dictionary in your face), or anyone who is over-dogmatic about which approach to dream interpretation should be used.

NIGHTMARES AND BAD DREAMS

ABOVE RUNNING FROM A PURSUER IS ONE OF THE MOST COMMON THEMES OF NIGHTMARES.

Most nightmares and bad dreams operate at both Level One and Level Two. It's perfectly possible to have a dream just at Level One about something unpleasant that has happened during the day, but for the most part bad dreams involve both a generalized Level One interpretation of how you see certain aspects of the world, and a deeper Level Two interpretation contained in the symbolism of the dream images themselves.

Nightmares take two obvious forms – dreams in which nasty things are done to you, and dreams in which you do nasty things to other people. We will look at each of these in turn.

NASTY THINGS DONE TO YOU

The most frequently reported dreams of this kind involve being chased – either by a human or mythical creature – often with the accompanying sensation of being unable to run to safety. Other reports include being trapped, being in prison awaiting execution, being shot at or knifed, being sexually abused, blinded, choked or mutilated. Often there is an overpowering sense of evil, and the dreamer wakes with all the physical and emotional reactions that would be there if the events were happening in waking life. At a lesser but still deeply unpleasant level there are dream experiences of being humiliated, scorned or thrust into harrowing or extremely stressful situations.

The first thing to emphasize about fearful dreams of this kind is that the fear lies in our reaction to them rather than in anything intrinsic to the dream itself. Odd as it may sound, the dream is still trying to be of use. The terrifying images it contains can be turned to our advantage if we know how – and can in the process be transformed, rather as the dog in the example on p.xxx turned from savaging the dreamer to licking her hand.

How is this done? Think back to the Senoi practice (*see* chapter 2) of rendering the dream harmless by facing the danger instead of running from it. But before you try this, it is important to interpret your nightmare just like any other dream. Use free association or amplification or role play to find out what it's trying to tell you. Usually its message has to do (at Level One) with the recognition of fears that you are unable to understand and come to terms with, and (at Level Two) with the actual cause of these fears. Level Two interpretation often reveals these fears to be prompted by some quality in yourself that has been repressed, and that now needs integrating into your mature personality.

The quality may be, for example, self-assertion, or determination, or your will to succeed. Because of early experiences in the home or the school you were perhaps taught that these things were unacceptable (because inconvenient) to the adults in your life, with the result not only that you were unable to develop them, but also that you felt guilty and afraid at their very existence. You defended against this guilt by denying them, pretending they were not there.

Now increasingly they are demanding recognition, a recognition that may be necessary for your further psychological development, but that reawakens your old fears about having something wild and imperfectly understood inside you.

An alternative possibility is that the dream represents some crisis or event in your life that you are afraid to face – something you need to master in order to express your personality more fully. It may be a task you have to perform, in connection, for example, with personal relationships or with your private or professional life.

Once you have identified the dream message, accepted the repressed quality in your personality and begun to integrate it into your conscious life, the nightmares will often cease of their own accord. Their purpose has been fullfiled. But if this doesn't happen, instruct your mind before going to sleep to turn and face your dream pursuer or stand up to your attackers. Sometimes this succeeds in turning the dream into a lucid one (*see* chapter 6), but even if this is not the case the message usually gets through remarkably easily to the dreaming mind. And once the danger is confronted, most people report that who or whatever was causing it becomes friendly or turns away or disappears.

If this method is used in conjunction with dream interpretation, the dream has fullfiled its purpose and given you its message. And you may find that dreams now come that are a friendly, non-frightening development of the nightmare. The nightmare dream characters or situations are transformed into allies, and interpretation of these new dreams may reveal further messages to you from your unconscious on the same theme but in a friendly form and coming from an even deeper level.

Facing your fear in a dream may also help you to be less fearful in waking life. I referred to this possibility in chapter 2, and many people spontaneously report that this happens (gains in self-confidence are also reported). And since dream emotions are physiologically every bit as real as waking emotions, there is no good psychological reason why it shouldn't.

NASTY THINGS DONE
TO SOMEBODY ELSE

Dreams in which you are doing unpleasant things to other people can be carrying the same message. Some aspect of yourself that needs expressing is currently being repressed, with the result (Level One interpretation) that you feel a great deal of undirected anger and frustration. Don't be worried that, as the dream is a violent one, this aspect must be to do with violence. The dream violence is usually to do with the strength of the frustration that this repressed part of you feels, rather than with its actual nature. Level Two interpretation may reveal this repressed part as nothing more than your creativity, or your individuality, or your desire to make a mark on the world.

In my experience, dreams of this kind also represent in some people a high level of free-floating anxiety. That is, the anxiety where we feel worried, depressed and ill-at-ease, or vaguely guilty and unhappy about ourselves, but without knowing quite why.

ABOVE FEELINGS OF ANXIETY MAY BE TRANSLATED INTO DREAMS IN WHICH WE BEHAVE BADLY TOWARDS OTHERS.

103

The unconscious is prone to dramatize this anxiety for us along the lines of 'Okay, I'm worried about something; what could it be? What's the worse possible thing I could be worried about? Killing someone? Must be that; okay, let's act it out.' The only problem is that with free-floating anxiety there isn't anything specific we are worrying about. It is an anxiety habit, either short term or long, into which we have slipped as a result of our previous life experiences.

Although the dream hasn't got the details of the message right, it has still performed a useful function. It's brought to the dreamer's attention the destructive effect of free-floating anxiety or of feelings of guilt, prompting him or her to let them go and to use the emotional and mental energy involved more productively.

Dreams in which nasty things are done to others but in which you are the observer rather than the actor seem for many people to fall into the same category. Again interpretation shows that the mind is often preoccupied by fear of catastrophe, but of a nameless, unspecified kind. The dream dramatizes a justification for this fear, thus allowing some of the emotion involved to be released, and brings to the attention of the waking mind the extent to which this fear is dominating and distorting your view of reality.

EMBARRASSING DREAMS

Though not as bad as nightmares, embarrassing dreams (often recurring ones), in which the dreamer is asked to make a speech or sit an examination for which they haven't prepared, or suddenly finds him or herself naked in public, often cause people great distress. The Level One interpretation is usually clear. The dreamer, although perhaps highly successful in waking life, nevertheless feels vulnerable and exposed. If we're honest, none of us are as sure of ourselves as we seem. Even if the world sees an expert, we're appalled sometimes by our lack of knowledge (surely there *must* be people who know more about the subject than me!) and frightened that we we'll prove inadequate, or that our ignorance will be exposed, or that our hard-won success will suddenly be taken from us.

Level Two interpretation will help us identify the source of this vulnerability. Perhaps parents who always expect too much from us as children. Perhaps traumatic experiences (again often in childhood) when our inexpertise our our lack of knowledge about something was cruelly exposed. Once the source is identified, the drams will often stop of their own accord.

Though public nakedness is often only a symbol of this general vulnerability, for some people dream interpreation traces it back to an over-prudish upbringing in which the human body was regarded as sinful, and the child's natural curiosity about his or her own and other people's bodies was insensitively punished and suppressed. Interpretation can also sometimes reveal feelings of sexual inadequacy, but this is not especially common. In addition to working on the interpretation of their public nakedness in dreams, I advise people (rather like facing their fears in a nightmare) actually to enjoy the nakedness. Where there is a link with punishment and guilt as a result of adult disapproval years ago of the dreamer's natural tendency to childhood exhibitionism, this switch from embarrassment to enjoyment helps release the repressed emotions. Subsequently, the nudity dreams may stop (rather to the dreamer's disappointment!).

USING THE LESSONS OF DREAMS

105

Once you have begun to interpret your dreams, the question arises, what do you do with the lessons you learn? I can't pursue this too far, as it takes us away from dreams and into the whole vast and rich area of psychotherapy itself. The dream rarely tells you what to do; it shows you the path but not how to tread it. However, by recognizing the path, by identifying the problem, the solution in turn often becomes clear to us. The dream may show us we need to be more open to others, or more sensitive, or more assertive, or that we need to lay to rest the ghosts of the past. Having recognized this, the way ahead becomes clearer, provided we have the courage and the motivation to follow it.

In using the lessons of dreams there are certain important guidelines to keep very much in mind:

• Don't be gullible. Dream interpretation is never an exact science. And dreams aren't always the fount of wisdom. Don't feel you must slavishly follow what the dream appears to teach you if this goes against common sense. Don't imagine the dream is always right and rational judgement always wrong. Use dreams in the way you would use advice from a knowledgeable and well-meaning friend. Sometimes the advice is good, sometimes good but impractical, and sometimes it misses the point.

• Attach more importance to advice gained from several dreams rather than from a single one (unless you're sure it is operating at Level Three).

• Keep monitoring your dreams. If you take advice from a dream, don't regard this as once and for all advice. Circumstances change, and the dream may well have something more to say on the subject a little later on.

ABOVE KEEP A NOTE OF ALL YOUR DREAMS SO THAT YOU CAN REFER BACK TO THEM AS THE CIRCUMSTANCES IN YOUR LIFE CHANGE.

• Look to your dreams for advice on matters relating to how you should face up to your own complexes, how you should develop your potential, how you should better integrate your conscious and unconscious lives, how you should express and handle your emotions, how you should give rein to your creativity, rather than for advice on how you should make specific decisions or on how the future is going to turn out.

One of the main lessons to be learnt from dream interpretation – or rather one of the benefits that arises from this interpretation – doesn't come from the specific advice dreams are able to give. It comes from the fact that through dreamwork you become more attuned over a period of time to your creative, intuitive self. Dreamwork leaves you

106

feeling more whole, more open to your emotions, often gentler and more understanding of yourself and others.

It can help men feel more in contact with the feminine side of their natures, and women more in contact with the masculine in theirs. Dreamwork gives you a deeper sense of yourself, a realization that much of your life takes place below the surface of your consciousness, that to live only in our rational, logical thoughts is to skate thinly over the waters of our being.

Dreamwork is free, open and readily available. It represents not an escape from reality but a movement into a wider, richer, more comprehensive reality. It asks little from us but time, patience, and the use of a few relatively simple techniques. And it repays us a thousand times over.

LUCID DREAMING

I t's time now to discuss a strange but widely reported phenomenon, the apparent ability of spiritually advanced men and women to remain conscious throughout the hours of sleep. Until we've experienced such a condition for ourselves we can't really know what it means, but accounts available to us suggest they inhabit a night-long dream world in which they are aware that they're dreaming, and able as a result to control the dream state and use it for spiritual growth, or for gaining information not available by normal means.

It is said that, either in the dream state or in out-of-the-body experiences (of which more shortly), such people are also able to project themselves to those who need them – their students, the sick, the unhappy. People who claim first-hand knowledge of these states tell me that after such visits both visitor and visited are often able the following morning to recount in the same kind of detail what actually happened.

Without aspiring to such feats, it is possible for most (probably all) of us to retain or regain consciousness during at least some of our dreaming moments. That is, to observe and control with our conscious minds the dream material served up by the unconscious. Dreams in which this

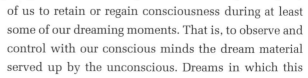

LEFT THE CHARACTERS IN LUCID DREAMS SEEM SOMEHOW MORE 'REAL' THAN IN WAKING LIFE.

conscious control operates are usually referred to as lucid dreams, and their characteristic is that when experiencing them one actually knows one is asleep and dreaming.

Lucid dreams have a particular quality to them that, once experienced, is not easily forgotten. The quality commences the moment when, in the middle of a dream, the realization dawns that 'Ah, I must be dreaming!' Most people find that, at this moment, the dream seems instantly to open out. Colours become more vivid, more vibrant. People and events, though one is now aware they are only part of a dream, seem paradoxically to become more real. And – this is the key element – the dreamer knows that the dream can be controlled. He or she can usually decide what to do and where to go. (I say 'usually' because it doesn't always work that way; in a lucid dream there is always an element of the unexpected; the final decisions are still in the hands of the dream itself.) Often it remains hard to hang on to this state. Sometimes one wakes. Sometimes the dream slips back into an ordinary dream. Sometimes it remains only intermittently lucid. Maddeningly, having had one lucid dream, the dreamer may have to wait weeks, months, perhaps years before experiencing another. On occasions, several lucid dreams may come together over a very short period, followed by a long fallow interval during which nothing happens. There seems no rhyme or reason about it. One tries a technique for lucid dreaming, and Eureka it works – perhaps for several nights running – then for no apparent reason it ceases to work, and one seems to be back where one started.

THE STRANGE QUALITY OF LUCID DREAMS

In lucid dreams one really is travelling in another world as objectively 'real' as this one – although one's mind is conscious and able to take decisions, the dream scenery and often the dream events are still sketched in by the secret, mysterious processes of the unconscious.

109

So if I decide in a lucid dream to visit a South Sea Island for example, I don't have to recall what such an island looks like, and then try and imagine it. The island is created for me, and turns out to be as full of surprises as a real place visited for the first time. It isn't even a clever amalgam of my past experiences, a set of permutations from my memory banks. It has all the appearance of a real place created not by my mind but by the hand of nature herself.

Even if I visit a familiar place in the dream, I don't have to construct the details consciously. The dream will do the constructing for me, down to the last detail, but with those subtle differences from waking life that are characteristic of non-lucid dreams. I may find two windows in a room where only one should exist, a door in a wall where in real life there is no door, a friend who looks older or younger, taller or shorter than they should. And no matter how striking these differences are to me, I may be unable to change them to fit the real facts of the matter.

I remember in a lucid dream finding myself in a strange street in a strange town. Everything was apparently normal, as in any normal street. There were shops, there were people; the only abnormal thing was that, unlike everyone else, I was involuntarily gliding along several centimetres above the pavement instead of using my feet. At first I wondered if other people would notice, then I realized I appeared to be invisible to them. As I passed two girls, something that trailed behind me, like a silk scarf, brushed against their faces, and they looked up puzzled and a little startled, as if half aware of a presence, yet unable to see what it was.

This and others of my lucid dreams illustrate the point I made earlier, namely that although one knows one is dreaming, the final decisions are still in the hands of the dream itself. So in my dream I found myself invisible to passers-by. My strong impression in the dream was that I was visiting some place that has objective existence, but I was there not as my waking self but in some kind of travelling, non-material body. The place I was visiting was obeying the laws of waking life; it was I who was breaking them.

FALSE AWAKENING

For some dreamers, there is an experience similar to lucid dreaming that we call false awakening. Instead of becoming aware that the dream is a dream, the dreamer dreams that he or she awakes – sometimes to the point of actually believing they are dressing, or are at the breakfast table telling the family about the dreams of the night. Thus the dreamer almost gains consciousness within the dream, but instead of the consciousness registering the fact of dreaming, it makes 'sense' of the experience by assuming it is fully awake. People who experience false awakenings are sometimes able to go on and develop the condition into full lucid dreaming.

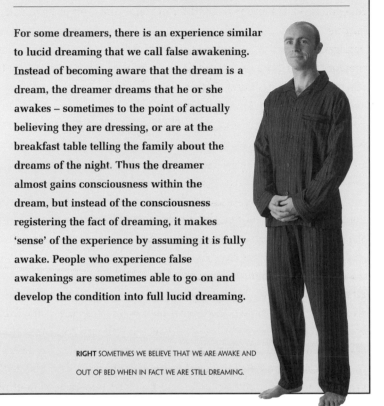

RIGHT SOMETIMES WE BELIEVE THAT WE ARE AWAKE AND OUT OF BED WHEN IN FACT WE ARE STILL DREAMING.

111

OUT-OF-THE-BODY EXPERIENCES

Just as false awakening may be a half-way stage towards lucid dreaming, so lucid dreams appear to be a half-way stage between normal dreaming and OBEs (out-of-the-body experiences). In an OBE one travels through familiar and unfamiliar scenery just as in a lucid dream, but the difference is that one is aware of what seems to be an actual physical separation from one's body.

OBEs can happen at times other than sleep; for example as a result of a sudden shock to the body, or when unconscious under anaesthetic, or when the heart has stopped beating and one is for a short time clinically dead (a so-called NDE or near-death experience). Experiences in dream OBEs seem to all intents and purposes to be the same as those that happen during these non-dreaming states, so for present purposes we can talk about dreaming and non-dreaming OBEs as if they are a single category.

So realistic is the feeling during an OBE that one is inhabiting a consciousness separate from one's physical body that one has the sensation of looking at the body from the outside, and may even struggle to re-enter it, fearing that death has occurred. The sense of realism in an OBE is often heightened by the fact that one can even notice things about the physical body that can't normally be seen while within it. For example, one of my students experienced an OBE while very ill and in a state of physical collapse. She saw herself placed on the stretcher and taken out of her house to the ambulance, and registered with a kind of detached interest 'Oh, so that's what my head and my hairstyle look like from the top!' Other people report similar experiences. Sometimes of floating along behind their physical bodies while out walking, and of seeing themselves from the back. Sometimes of seeing things that others are doing to them (a common experience during clinical death, when after recovery the patient sometimes describes to doctors and nurses elements of the treatment he or she received that apparently they could not have known by normal means).

Many spiritual and occult traditions have long taught that in OBEs, the soul or astral body (call it what you will) actually does leave the physical body, and is free to travel both in this world and in the astral realms, and recent medical research into NDEs lends support to at least the first part of this conviction. Others doubt it, however, and claim the OBE is simply the way the imagination works under certain unusual sets of circumstances. My own approach is to ask people how OBE experiences seemed to them at the time, before the rational mind had a chance to step in and try to make 'sense' of them. There are dangers in insisting too swiftly that the experiences people have are not what they themselves take them to be. Where experiences are deeply personal, the subject's own interpretation of them isn't necessarily inferior to that of the 'expert' trying to rationalize them away from the outside.

If we ask people to interpret their own OBEs, they often express the conviction that the experience was exactly what it appeared to be. Namely that some part of their consciousness left the physical body and was temporarily located outside it. In this sense, the OBE is in contrast both with ordinary dreams and lucid dreams. No matter how realistic the dream, we are sure on waking that it was only a dream. Whereas after the OBE the feeling remains, often undimmed years later, that consciousness can exist outside the physical body, and that the knowledge of this fact changes one's beliefs about both the nature of life and the nature of death.

LUCID DREAMS AND OBEs

As to the connection between lucid dreams and OBEs, in one of my first experiences of lucid dreams I told myself that I wanted to fly. I was immediately and to my great surprise thrown on my back and propelled, head first and at great speed, through a black space, like a very dark night. At the same moment I heard a rushing, roaring noise inside my head and my whole body vibrated (inwardly rather than physically) at a very high frequency. It was the first time I had experienced the phenomenon, but I found myself saying, still asleep; 'I know what's going to happen; I'm going to leave my body.' Though not particularly frightened, I thought it sensible to say a prayer for protection. The instant I did so, as if a switch had been thrown, the experience ended.

Checking up later I found I was correct in recognizing that the rushing noise and the feeling of vibration are reported by many writers as a frequent prelude to an OBE.

MEDITATION

The benefits of meditation at both psychological and spiritual levels are many and far-reaching. From the point of view of dreaming the most important of these are that the regular practice of meditation (daily if possible), as it:

• Improves your concentration, thus allowing you to be more aware during both waking and sleeping of what is going on in your own mind.
• Improves access to your unconscious.

A short period of meditation last thing at night is one of the best ways of giving you more access to your creativity, and in particular to the creative world of dreams. Choose as quiet a place as possible, and sit on an upright chair or cross-legged on the floor. To begin with, five minutes of meditation is enough. As your practice progresses, so you will find this period tends to extend of its own accord until it stretches to 20 minutes or so. Lower the eyelids so that you are aware of only a narrow band of unfocused light, or close your eyes completely if you prefer (and can still keep awake).

RIGHT MEDITATION WILL IMPROVE CONCENTRATION AND ACCESS TO THE UNCONSCIOUS MIND.

114

The aim in meditation is to keep the mind alert yet relaxed, and focused upon a single stimulus rather than upon the ceaseless chatter of your thoughts.

A good stimulus to choose is your breathing. Put your awareness in the gentle rise and fall of your abdomen, or at the place in your nostrils where you feel the air cool as you breathe in and warm as you breathe out. Count each out breath silently from one to 10, and when you get to 10 go back again to one.

Don't try to push away the thoughts that arise during this practice, but don't attend to them and don't follow them. Let each one enter and leave the mind while you simply concentrate upon the breathing.

An alternative point of focus is the point just above and between the eyes, the 'third eye' of yoga philosophy, and it helps if you can visualize a white light there.

As you practise meditation regularly and as your concentration improves, you can place at your point of concentration the idea that your consciousness will flow easily and smoothly from waking into sleep. Repeat this as a formula of words if you like, though if you can it's better to hold it as an abstract idea, or like the idea of a journey that flows smoothly and uninterruptedly from waking through sleep and into reawaking tomorrow morning.

When you finish the meditation, keep the mind in this calm and tranquil state. It's best to go straight to bed. Keep your physical movements unhurried, as if they are flowing in harmony with your consciousness.

When you settle to sleep, allow your awareness to rest gently in the same place as your meditation.

Meditation is a major subject in its own right, and I have only had space here to touch on one or two of the issue that help most with our dreaming,

INDUCING LUCID DREAMS

Since lucid dreams have such a special quality about them, people naturally ask if there are ways in which they can be deliberately induced. The answer is that there are helpful techniques, but as in other dreamwork, patience is the watchword. You may practise a technique for weeks, months on end with no sign you're any nearer your goal. And then suddenly and unexpectedly, one night it happens. Keep the mind light, almost playful, as if you don't really care whether you lucid dream or not.

One of the most helpful techniques is meditation (*see* box, p.114). There are many systems of meditation, but the principle under-pinning them all is that they give the mind a point of focus – the mind is held on an object of concentration, whether it be the breath, a mantra, a visualization or whatever. Through practising in this way the mind becomes calmer and stiller, more aware of what is going on within it, and therefore better able to know the difference between waking and sleeping consciousness.

Some of the improved powers of concentration that come from meditation seem thus to carry over into sleep itself, and to help with the second technique, which is to train yourself to recognize the anomalies and illogicalities that occur in dreaming. Once you recognize these anomalies instead of accepting them without question (as we usually do in dreaming), you reach the point of recognizing 'Ah, so this must be a dream!' This recognition is one of the main ways of launching yourself into lucid dreaming.

For example, in one of my lucid dreams I was standing in a busy shopping street in what I knew for some reason was Britain, but when I looked at the names above the shops I saw they were in French. At once the realization dawned on me that anomalies such as French names above all the shops in a British high street only occur in dreams, and that therefore I was adrift in the dream world.

The alertness needed to recognize the strangeness of the goings-on in a dream and therefore to realize we are dreaming seems so easy to our daytime mind, yet once asleep we accept the most bizarre and unlikely happenings as a commonplace. So to lucid dream, we must . find ways of carrying some of our daytime alertness into sleep. As I've just said a few minutes meditation, in which the mind observes its own mental processes, helps. But a second technique is to ask yourself as often as possible during the day how you know you're not dreaming *now*. This instant.

How do you know? Is it because things happen predictably? Or is it because objects remain stable instead of undergoing strange metamorphoses? Or is it because you can take decisions and carry them out? Is is because you aren't constantly doing odd things such as flying, or shooting people or appearing nude in public?

By frequently reality testing of this kind, you train your mind to be more aware when things don't behave as they should, with the result that you leave yourself better equipped to notice the tell-tale unreality of the dream.

A third technique is to tell yourself, as you go off to sleep, that you're going to recognize your dreams for what they are. Repeat over and over again a set formula of words such as 'I'll know that I'm dreaming', and at the same time *imagine* yourself knowing this. Imagine yourself looking objectively at dream events, spotting the anomalies and realizing exactly what is going on. Help yourself further by thinking, during the day, of your consciousness as a continuous process stretching over the 24 hours instead of suspending itself during sleep. In this way you come to see waking events and dream events as parts of a continuum, rather than as separate categories of experience. A continuum in which you remain as attentive and aware during sleeping as during waking.

A fourth technique is to give yourself a task to do somewhere in the house while you're asleep, and focus your mind upon it during the day and last thing at night. One exercise I use in dream workshops is to tell participants to request someone at home to write down four numbers on a piece of paper for them, seal it in an envelope, and place it conspicuously on a table downstairs. When dreaming, the

117

task is to go downstairs, open the envelope and read the number.

I often angle the task towards ESP (extra sensory perception). There is no sense in which (unless they are sleepwalking) they will be able actually to open the physical envelope. But they might, in dreams, be able to open a kind of ESP equivalent of the envelope and read the contents. From an ESP point of view, the main problem is that although some individuals do indeed find the envelope and read the number in dreams, unless they are awakened there and then – as in a dream laboratory – the memory of the number is too vague to be much use the following morning. But from the point of view of lucid dreaming, the exercise often produces rapid results.

A variant on this technique, which again employs the notion of a task, is to leave a glass of drinking water in the bathroom, and then eat very salty food before retiring. In the night one feels thirsty but, since the body is reluctant to awake and actually go to the bathroom, the journey there becomes incorporated into a dream, and the awareness that this is happening reminds one that a dream is taking place. Another variant is to drink plenty of liquid so that in the night one wants to get up and empty the bladder; again the journey is done in a dream, and brings the realization that a dream is taking place.

Sometimes we realize we're dreaming for reasons other than a recognition of the strangeness of the dream world. For example, in

one of my dreams I was standing in the street looking up at the wording written around a clock face in the tower of a stone building. Finding myself able to read the words I thought to myself 'That's funny, usually in dreams you can't read things', and this was enough to prompt me to realize that 'yes, of course, this is a dream!'.

LEFT TRY TO MAKE YOURSELF DREAM ABOUT THE REFRESHING GLASS OF WATER THAT YOU HAVE LEFT IN THE BATHROOM.

A technique used by Native Americans that also relies upon sharpened concentration in waking life is to close your eyes and regularly try to visualize your hands. Tell yourself as you do so that you will see your hands in your dream, and that when you do you will know you are dreaming.

One final technique. When remembering your dreams each morning, look for illogicalities. Ask yourself why these weren't enough to tell you that you were dreaming. Convince yourself that next time these sorts of things will be quite enough to make you realize you're dreaming.

ABOVE BECOME AWARE THAT YOU ARE DREAMING BY TEACHING YOURSELF THAT THE SIGHT OF YOUR HANDS IN A DREAM IS A SIGN THAT YOU ARE DREAMING.

119

The more familiar you become with your dream world, the more likely you are to recognize it for what it is and allow it to become lucid.

Help matters further by reflecting upon your dreams with the same quality of mind you use to reflect upon waking events. Run them through in your mind, like any other set of memories. Try and recall the texture of them, not simply the events themselves. Tell yourself that in future dreams you must revisit the places remembered from past dreams, in just the way you can revisit places in waking life. Own your dreams, in the way you own the rest of your experience.

ENDWORD

CHAPTER SEVEN

Certain questions arise time and time again when readers and callers to phone-in programmes ask me for information about dreaming. I will conclude by looking at the three most frequent topics.

The first one concerns recurring dreams. People of all ages report having the same dream over and over again, often over a period of many years, and they wonder if there is any particular significance in this. The answer is yes, for two main reasons. The first is that recurring dreams further weaken the argument that dreams are merely a consequence of the brain's dumping unwanted material during sleep, rather as computers discard unwanted information when we exit from a program. Recurring dreams clearly indicate that the material concerned is not 'unwanted', and relates to issues firmly established in the mind.

The second reason for the significance of recurring dreams is that they indicate there are matters deserving particular attention in the dreamer's psychological life. The dream is repeatedly attempting to draw attention to these matters, perhaps because they have to do with an area of life or of psychological potential that the dreamer is neglecting, or because they relate to old anxieties or concerns that have not yet been laid to rest. Alternatively, the dream may be trying to provide guidance as to long-term life-goals, or the particular path that will prove best for the dreamer concerned. Interestingly, recurring dreams sometimes involve a place (typically a house) that

ABOVE THE SAME IMAGES WILL OFTEN OCCUR AGAIN AND AGAIN IN OUR DREAMS.

121

the dreamer has never visited in waking life, but which is seen in such detail, and is so consistent in appearance, that the dreamer is haunted by a sense of its objective reality. Sometimes he or she may actually go searching for it when awake, and not surprisingly wonders if the dream could be precognitive, or perhaps an echo of a previous life. The answer is, of course, that recurring dreams are no less symbolic than ordinary dreams. The place (particularly if it is a house) may thus represent the dreamer, and the dream may be showing that there are large areas of the self that still remain to be discovered, or that for some reason the dreamer is not allowing the real self to be fully expressed.

ABOVE SOMETIMES OUR DECEASED LOVED ONES LOOK MORE BEAUTIFUL IN OUR DREAMS.

Another question that often crops up has to do with meeting in dreams people who have died. Sometimes such people look exactly as the dreamer remembered them, at other times they seem younger, or more beautiful, or restored to full health and vigour. Sometimes they give messages, often of comfort and reassurance, concerning both their continuing existence, and the future well-being and happiness of the dreamer.

It is all too easy to dismiss these dreams as wishful thinking, particularly if the dreamer was close to the person who has died, and has experienced a strong sense of loss and sadness. But my question to the dreamer is always, 'How do you feel about the experience? It is your dream: what do you think was happening?' Such a question is highly relevant. It is absurd to suppose that modern humankind has somehow 'proved' there is no life after death. At worst we simply don't know whether life goes on after the death of the physical body, and at best we have some very suggestive evidence (from near-death experiences, from the communications of mediums, and from the teachings of the great spiritual traditions) that it does. Thus if the dreamer feels convinced that someone who has died was communicating in their dream, then this may very well be the case.

I am also sometimes asked about the devices currently coming on the market for inducing lucid dreams, and about whether they really work. The answer is that there is no guarantee. They function by noting those changes in breathing pattern or brain rhythms or eye movements that signal the sleeper has entered dreaming sleep, and they administer some small stimulus (such as a very mild electric shock), which is in theory sufficient to alert the dreamer to the fact that he or she is dreaming, but insufficient to produce awakening. For some people, this seems to be effective (although they may have to practise with the device for some weeks first); for others it is less so. The interested reader can learn more about this approach in K. Hearne's *The Dream Machine*. By all means try one of these devices if you like. They have been developed by serious scientists after careful research.

Ideally, however, lucid dreaming should arise spontaneously as the mind develops its powers through meditation and the other techniques . There is a risk that a short cut into lucid dreaming could be nothing more than a device for making your dream life more exciting. Valuable as this may be, it may not lead to deeper levels of inner understanding. Lucid dreaming should at best be seen as a sign of psycho-spiritual progress, rather than as an end in itself.

It would be wrong to end by wishing you only sweet dreams. Dreams are part of life itself, and life inevitably contains its bitter moments as well as its sweet ones. It would be unrealistic to pretend otherwise. Let me end this book, however, by wishing you wisdom in your dreams and the patience in your waking life to follow the path of that wisdom.

FURTHER READING

Boss, M. *I Dreamt Last Night*, Gardner Press, 1977.

Brook, S. *The Oxford Book of Dreams*, Oxford University Press, 1987.

Crookall, R. *More Astral Projections*, Aquarian, 1964.

Fontana, D. *The Secret Language of Dreams*, Pavilion Books (UK) and Chronicle (USA), 1994.

Fontana, D. *Teach Yourself to Dream*, Mitchell Beazley, 1977.

Fox, O. *Astral Projection*, University Books, 1962.

Freud, S. *The Interpretation of Dreams*, Penguin, 1976.

Garfield, P. G. *The Healing Power of Dreams,* Simon and Schuster, New York, 1991.

Green, C. E. *Lucid Dreams*, Hamish Hamilton, 1968.

Hearne, K. *The Dream Machine*, Aquarian Press, 1990.

Hutin, S. *History of Alchemy*, Tower, 1962.

Jung, C. *Dream Analysis*, Routledge, 1984.

LaBerg, S. and Rheingold, H. *Exploring the World of Lucid Dreaming*, Ballantine, New York, 1990.

Mavromatis, A. *Hypnogogia: The Unique State of Consciousness between Waking and Sleeping*, Routledge, 1987.

Monroe, R. *Journeys Out of the Body*, Corgi, 1974.

Moody, R. and Perry, P. *The Light Beyond: The Transforming Power of Near Death Experiences*, Pan, 1989.

Muldoon, S. and Carrington, H. *The Projection of the Astral Body,* Rider, 3rd Edition, 1968.

Perls, F. *Gestalt Therapy Verbatim*, Bantam, 1971.

Peterson, R. *Out of Body Experiences*, Charlottesville VA, Hampton Road, 1997.

Regardie, I. *The Tree of Life: A Study in Magic*, Samuel Weiser, 1972.

Rinbochay, L. and Hopkins, J. *Death, Intermediate State and Re-birth in Tibetan Buddhism*, Snow Lion, 1980.

Ullman, M. and Zimmerman, N. *Working With Dreams*, Aquarian Press, 1987.

Van de Castle, R. L. *Our Dreaming Mind*, Aquarian Press, 1994.

INDEX

127

LOOK AT LIFE...
with a NEW PERSPECTIVE

A series of comprehensive introductions
to key mind, body, spirit subjects

★ STYLISH AND ACCESSIBLE ★

★ STRAIGHTFORWARD AND PRACTICAL ★

★ CONTEMPORARY TWO COLOUR DESIGN WITH ILLUSTRATIONS ★

BOOKS AVAILABLE IN THE SERIES:

ISBN 1 86204 629 8

ISBN 1 86204 630 1

ISBN 1 86204 667 0

ISBN 1 86204 628 X

ISBN 1 86204 664 6

ISBN 1 86204 663 8

ISBN 1 86204 626 3

ISBN 1 86204 627 1

ISBN 1 86204 668 9

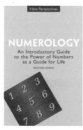

ISBN 1 86204 625 5

ISBN 1 86204 665 4

ISBN 1 86204 673 5

EACH BOOK: £5.99, PAPERBACK, 128 PAGES, 198 X 129MM